DAMIEN RYAN trained and worked as a journalist in the early 1990s, graduating from the University of Technology in Sydney, before moving into the theatre industry where he has worked professionally since 1995, as an actor, director and writer. He founded Sport for Jove Theatre Co. in 2009, and has worked for Bell Shakespeare for 15 years, along with Belvoir St Theatre and Sydney Theatre Company. His theatre work has received many awards. He has also worked and lectured for many years in the education sector in Australia, at secondary and tertiary levels. Damien has been a proud member of the MEAA for 23 years.

Andrea Demetriades as Antigone in Sport For Jove's 2016 production of Antigone. *(Photo: David McCarthy)*

ANTIGONE
& CYRANO DE BERGERAC

TWO ADAPTATIONS FOR
SPORT FOR JOVE BY
DAMIEN RYAN

Currency Press,
Sydney

CURRENCY PLAYS

First published in 2017
by Currency Press
Gadigal Land, Suite 310, 46-56 Kippax Street, Surry Hills NSW 2010
enquiries@currency.com.au
www.currency.com.au

Copyright: Introductions © Damien Ryan, 2017; *Cyrano de Bergerac* © Damien Ryan, 2013, 2017; *Antigone* © Damien Ryan, 2016, 2017.

COPYING FOR EDUCATIONAL PURPOSES

The Australian *Copyright Act 1968* (Act) allows a maximum of one chapter or 10% of this book, whichever is the greater, to be copied by any educational institution for its educational purposes provided that that educational institution (or the body that administers it) has given a remuneration notice to Copyright Agency Limited (CAL) under the Act.

For details of the CAL licence for educational institutions contact CAL, 11/66 Goulburn Street, Sydney, NSW, 2000; tel: within Australia 1800 066 844 toll free; outside Australia 61 2 9394 7600; fax: 61 2 9394 7601; email: info@copyright.com.au

COPYING FOR OTHER PURPOSES

Except as permitted under the Act, for example a fair dealing for the purposes of study, research, criticism or review, no part of this book may be reproduced, stored in a retrieval system, or transmitted in any form or by any means without prior written permission. All enquiries should be made to the publisher at the address above.

Any performance or public reading of *Cyrano de Bergerac* or *Antigone* is forbidden unless a licence has been received from the author or the author's agent. The purchase of this book in no way gives the purchaser the right to perform the plays in public, whether by means of a staged production or a reading. All applications for public performance should be addressed to the author c/- Sport for Jove Theatre Company, 38 Woodlands Street, Baulkham Hills, Sydney, 2153, Australia; damien.ryan@sportforjove.com.au

Cataloguing-in-publication data for this title is available from the National Library of Australia website: www.nla.gov.au

Typeset by Dean Nottle for Currency Press.
Cover design by Emma Vine for Currency Press.

Currency Press acknowledges the Traditional Owners of the Country on which we live and work. We pay our respects to all Aboriginal and Torres Strait Islander Elders, past and present.

Contents

ANTIGONE	1
Introduction	145
Act One	155
Act Two	196
CYRANO DE BERGERAC	1
Introduction	3
Act One	13
Act Two	45
Act Three	78
Act Four	104
Act Five	128

From left: Scott Sheridan as Pastrycook, Yalin Ozucelik as Cyrano, Barry French as Fourth Poet, Robert Jago as First Poet, Francesca Savige as Third Poet, John Turnbull as Rageneau (standing), Damien Strouthos as Poet, Madeleine Jones as Poet, Tim Walter as Poet and Julian Garner as Second Poet in Sport For Jove's 2013 production of Cyrano de Bergerac. *(Photo: Seiya Taguchi)*

SPORT FOR JOVE
THEATRE CO.

Company Manager	Steven Tait
Finance Director	Gai Strouthos
Chairperson	Gordon Stalley
Managing Artistic Director	Damien Ryan

Sport for Jove's production of *Cyrano de Bergerac* was the winner of three Sydney Theatre Awards in 2013: Best Independent Production, Best Actor and Best Director

Sport for Jove's production of *Antigone* was the winner of seven Sydney Theatre Awards in 2016: Best Independent Production, Best Actor, Best Actress, Best Director, Best Set Design, Best Costume Design, and Best Lighting Design.

Lizzie Schebesta as Roxane and Yalin Ozucelik as Cyrano in Sport For Jove's 2013 production of CYRANO DE BERGERAC. *(Photo: Seiya Taguchi)*

CYRANO
DE BERGERAC

A NEW ADAPTATION BY
DAMIEN RYAN
FROM THE ORIGINAL BY
EDMOND ROSTAND

*For Bernadette—
and the whole cast of dreamers and astronauts
who ever took up this mad adventure called theatre*

INTRODUCTION

This adaptation of *Cyrano de Bergerac* was originally inspired by Sean O'Shea, whose years of extraordinary performances have meant so much to me as an audience member and a colleague.

Originally staged in 1897, this play's celebration of theatricality and conviction to entertain is exhilarating, hence its ongoing popularity and its almost continuous success around the world.

Cyrano remains relevant now for the same reasons Shakespeare does—its ideas and concerns are simply and profoundly human. What does individualism mean, and how do we protect and serve our personal vision of the world without compromise? How do we remain faithful to what we believe in? What is love and what happens to love when we get past its clichés and false ideals? How does self-esteem define us all our lives? What is beauty? What drives male aggression? What is courage? For Rostand, *Cyrano* was a passionate plea for a France that he felt was losing its soul, its romance and its creativity: return to a more enlightened, brave and individual sense of identity—to something with panache.

Rostand was hurt into writing this play by losing faith in the country he lived in. 1897 was in the early-to-mid period of La Belle Epoque—the 'beautiful era'—however, as with any apparently 'golden age', it did not necessarily feel that way to the struggling artists at its centre, who were as condemned as they were celebrated for their revolutionary artistic visions. For Rostand, France (and Paris particularly) was becoming a petty political and economic slave to the ideals of others: politically corrupt, cruel, in danger of losing its leadership and idealism, and forgetting its past and the lessons of memory. Cyrano is France—fighting to keep its plume in the air. The play is about so much more than love, despite being one of the great love stories in theatre history. It has a powerful and contagious philosophy of living up to one's principles, of courage, and of selfless sacrifice.

At the centre of that philosophy is individualism: the defining theme of the whole realist movement of the late 1800s and early 1900s, coinciding with Rostand writing *Cyrano*. Rostand (like Ibsen, Chekhov and Shaw at that same artistic moment) wanted to explore the concept of a powerful individual spirit crushed by an irreconcilable sense of being different to the world around oneself, an inability to find a way to live satisfactory to one's sense of right and wrong, or commensurate to one's philosophy of self-expression. This struggle is central in plays like *Hedda Gabler*, *Miss Julie*, *A Doll's House* and much of Chekhov's work. But Rostand wrote a play that goes well beyond the strict bounds of realism. *Cyrano de Bergerac* is mythical in its size and scale—part nineteenth-century pictorialism, part fairytale, part melodrama, part Shakespearean epic, and certainly part realist, with its deep psychological motivations, complex ideals and the withholding of an enormous life-changing secret by the central character.

It makes a powerful point about the whole genre of romance and its failure in the real world. Only together do Cyrano and Christian make the perfect man: attractive and brilliant, sensitive and strong, physically sensual and intellectually powerful, full of blood and full of tears (as the 'last letter' embodies in Act Five). It takes the two of them to be a great romantic hero, and we watch a woman's futile search for that hero somewhere between them. *Cyrano de Bergerac* is filled with symmetries to Hamlet and Romeo and Juliet, but this time, very wittily, there are two Romeos beneath Juliet's balcony. The play has wonderful things to say about the value of poetry to express things that cannot be easily expressed: emotional things, real things. But it also asks us how far poetry can really go in describing the deepest human feelings.

Cyrano and Roxane provide the pivotal relationship. The overarching story is of them remaining faithful to each other all their lives, neither experiencing sex or sensual pleasure, living in adoration of each other without realising it until it is too late. In that sense the play is like a Greek myth, but with a deliriously funny core. It was a joy to adapt it and to play with this wonderful group of actors in our first season in 2013, led by the brilliant Yalin Ozucelik and Lizzie Schebesta—actors whose souls Cyrano himself would have admired.

> CYRANO: You see it, but you'll never have this plume,
>   It soars above the battle's mud and ash,
>   It stays with me, one thing …
> ROXANE: [*kissing him*] … this!
> CYRANO: *My panache!*

Rostand's original is in Alexandrine 12-syllable rhyming verse, the dominant form in French poetry for several centuries. I have used rhyming and blank verse in iambic pentameter (10-syllable lines), along with some prose. I have sought to serve Rostand's intentions at every point through structure, poetic tone, meaning and intention and am indebted to the many fine translations produced in the past 120 years. This is, however, a new text and I am equally indebted to the cast and creative team for their input and guidance.

The only significant departure we have made is from Rostand's intended setting—Paris in 1640 under Louis XIII, which was the era of the real Cyrano de Bergerac. Rostand's play uses a swashbuckling caped crusader of the musketeer era, so rich in form, silhouette and style, but also so extremely familiar to us, the setting almost cartoonish in its well-established iconography. We have brought the era forward for several reasons, some interpretive, some purely practical. Regarding the latter, it is simply impossible for an independent Australian theatre company to afford to effectively costume the play in keeping with the excess required of 1640s Paris.

We have brought the setting forward 300 years in time. Why? The new setting is in keeping with the original's heightened vision of fashion, art, style, letter-writing, 'Frenchness', grand pictorial theatre and the brutal onset of catastrophic war. But more fundamentally, I wanted Cyrano to be a soldier in the rawest sense, in the modern world of mechanised war. Not a cartoonish swordsman in a long cape, but a figure we can recognise: a gritty, bruised and very real military poet, a chaotic Wilfred Owen, a voice in the wilderness, still a swordsman, still larger than life, leading a band of very real soldiers in the brutal and degrading warzone. The original play's links to World War I are remarkable—*Cyrano de Bergerac* was described in the wake of World War I as 'the play that got us through the war'. It was performed many times across France during the conflict, literally intended to ignite national pride and inspire a beleaguered people. The play's Fourth Act depicts the savage Siege of Arras, fought in 1640. It was hugely significant to the French people that the very same patch of ground in Arras was again the scene of a brutal siege and battle in World War I. We have replaced the Spanish enemy with the Prussian army, unified into the German army with the abolition of the monarchies in 1918.

The *précieuses* of 1640, of which the real Roxane was a member, were groups of remarkable women demanding the right to education and literacy, determined to live for poetry, art, linguistic decadence and the right for women to meet in private as men could. They bear some striking resemblances to the forward-thinking suffragette movement of the early twentieth century, another portrait I thought more palpable to a contemporary audience.

There is a leap of two decades between Act One and Act Five. To move from 1913 to the 1930s brings a wonderfully clear sense of change and the passage of time, and of course brings the weight of another catastrophic conflict (World War II) with it. Cyrano, the self-destructive soldier-poet, goes on living in a world bent on destroying itself.

Rostand was using a bygone era to allegorise his own period. I too have stepped back 100 years from my own period, to consider the play through the perspective of Rostand's world, which would come to be considered the definitive epoch of French achievement and panache—in no small part due to *Cyrano de Bergerac*.

The Real Cyrano of History

The real Cyrano was born in Paris in 1619, the son of a lawyer. He moved just outside the city to the small fief of Bergerac with his family while aged three. He bore no real relation to the town of Bergerac in Gascony, on the Dordogne, though the town sells his big-nosed postcard to this day. He indeed had a largish nose, mocked and adored by his friends, but nothing like Rostand's symbolic exaggeration.

Cyrano met his lifelong friend, Henri Le Bret, as a young student. Le Bret would posthumously publish Cyrano's poetry and works in 1657, a final act of love to his best friend. Cyrano was a fearsome and quarrelsome soldier, often given to duelling, who joined Carbon de Castel Jaloux's company of guards for the Thirty Years War. He was wounded at Arras and retired to studies and writing in 1641.

Le Bret wrote that Cyrano had always been 'distant with women'. Other poets labelled him a homosexual and a *libertin*. While his life was impoverished and dissolute, his writing was witty, elegant and literary, but too full of invective to bring him popularity—although Molière stole scenes from his play *Le Pédant Joué*. Cyrano's great work, the tragedy *La Mort d'Agrippine*, was removed from the stage as it caused a scandal. Cyrano died in 1655 when a wooden beam fell from a window onto his head as he entered his patron's house. He was just 35 years old.

Roxane and Christian have historical counterparts too—Madeleine Robineau, a distant cousin of Cyrano, married Christophe de Neuvillette, who died at Arras. Madeleine lived out her later days at a convent in Paris. Rostand's version of Roxane amalgamates Madeleine with Marie Robineau, a *précieuse* who took the nickname of Roxane after the name of the woman who stole the heart of Alexander the Great.

Other figures are drawn from history too. Ragueneau was a baker and poet who would later work for Molière. Lignière was a drunken poet who actually did involve Cyrano in a fight against almost impossible odds. Cyrano's most significant work, *Etats et Empires de la Lune*, is used in Act Three as Cyrano fools De Guiche with his voyage to the moon. It is considered the first piece of science fiction in human history—the tale of a man who journeys through the moon and the sun—a fitting metaphor for a life of futile but transcendent aspiration.

Edmond Rostand

Rostand was born to a wealthy family on April Fools' Day in 1868. He studied law, and after a failed publication of poetry, turned to the stage in 1894 with a witty rewrite of *Romeo and Juliet* called *Les Romanesques*, which later became a long-running musical. His obsession with *Romeo and Juliet* would also inspire *Cyrano de Bergerac* in 1897: his fourth play and first success. Perhaps success is an understatement: it was an overwhelming triumph, one of the most immediate theatrical hits in history, playing over 1,000 consecutive performances with the great Coquelin in the role of Cyrano, and extolling Rostand as the new Victor Hugo. He would go on to write unsuccessful plays for the great actor Sarah Bernhardt, and his romantic style did not survive against the fierce, stern and less facile movement of Naturalism sweeping Europe. But *Cyrano* has remained among the most popular plays of all time. Rostand died of pneumonia, aged 50, after catching a cold during the Armistice celebrations in 1918. Cyrano's final revenge—his famed biographer catching a sniffle.

Damien Ryan
May 2017

Cyrano de Bergerac was first produced by Sport for Jove at Sydney Hills Shakespeare in the Park Festival, Sydney, on 14 December 2013, with the following cast:

CYRANO DE BERGERAC	Yalin Ozucelik
ROXANE	Lizzie Schebesta
CHRISTIAN DE NEUVILLETTE	Scott Sheridan
DUENNA / MOTHER MARGUERITE	Vanessa Downing
MONTFLEURY / CARBON / POET	Barry French
LE BRET / PASTRYCOOK / POET	Julian Garner
PATRON / ACTOR / POET / CADET	Robert Jago
BUFFET GIRL / PASTRYCOOK / POET / PAGE / SISTER MARTHA	Madeleine Jones
DE GUICHE / ACTOR / PASTRYCOOK / POET	James Lugton
LISE / JODELET / SISTER CLAIRE	Bernadette Ryan
BOY	Max Ryan
STREET KID	Oliver Ryan
MARQUISE / PASTRYCOOK / POET / SISTER CLAIRE	Francesca Savige
PICKPOCKET / ACTOR / PASTRYCOOK / POET / CADET	Christopher Stalley
LIGNERE / PASTRYCOOK / POET / CADET	Damien Strouthos
BELLEROSE / MUSKETEER / CAPUCHIN / SENTINEL	Christopher Tomkinson
RAGENEAU	John Turnbull
VALVERT / ACTOR / PASTRYCOOK / POET / CADET	Tim Walter

Director, Damien Ryan
Set Designer, Barry French
Costume Designer, Anna Gardiner
Lighting Designer, Toby Knyvett
Sound Designer, David Stalley
Fight Choreographer, Scott Witt
Technical Manager, Jeremy Page
Production Manager, Jess Penny
Stage Manager, Lija Simpson
Assistant Stage Managers, Katherine Holmes, Lauren Holmes and Rebecca Poulter

CHARACTERS

CYRANO (Hercule-Savinien de Cyrano de Bergerac), a Gascon soldier
ROXANE (Madeleine Robin)
CHRISTIAN DE NEUVILLETTE, a soldier from Touraine
LE BRET (Vidame de Malgouyre Estressac Lesbas d'Escarabiot), a Cadet
RAGUENEAU, a pastry chef
LISE, wife to Ragueneau
DE GUICHE, commander of the French armies
VALVERT, a presidential cavalry officer
LIGNIERE, a drunk poet
DUENNA, guardian to Roxane
CARBON DE CASTEL-JALOUX, captain of the Gascony Cadets
CADETS, Gascon soldiers:
    Baron de Peyrescous de Colignac
    Baron Jean de Casterac de Cahuzac
    Chevalier Albert d'Antignac-Juzet
    Baron Hillot de Blagnac-Salechan de Castel Crabioules
SENTINEL
MUSKETEER
CAPUCHIN, a friar
MOTHER MARGUERITE
SISTER MARTHA
SISTER CLAIRE
Punters of theatre: TROOPERS, BURGHERS, LACKEYS, PAGES, MARQUISES, PATRONS, CHILD, PICKPOCKET, STREET KID
Theatre staff: BELLEROSE, BUFFET GIRL, MUSICIANS, MONTFLEURY, JODELET, other ACTORS
POETS
PASTRYCOOKS

Many character entries and exits can be decided at the director's discretion. This play is shaped by the parameters of a chosen space, and by the production's intention. This is particularly relevant to the tableau scenes, which can have many or just a few characters onstage at once. For example, in the first production's opening scene, the PICKPOCKET was planted in the audience—in later productions they were hidden in a huge drape of curtains to burst out at a key moment.

This play can be performed by a cast as small as nine, or by a much bigger cast.

SETTING

It is late 1913. The story spans World War I. Act One takes place on stage at the Hotel de Bourgogne in Paris. Act Two is in Ragueneau's bakery the next morning. Act Three is in the Marais, at the house of Roxane several months later, in 1914. Act Four moves to Arras in 1917, with soldiers holed up in a besieged camp. Act Five moves to the Parisian convent of the Sisters of Mercy in the early 1930s, before the outbreak of World War II.

*Above: Lizzie Schebesta as Roxane and Scott Sheridan as Christian.
Below; from left: Yalin Ozucelik as Cyrano, Robert Jago as Actor, Francesca Savige as Marquise, Madeleine Jones as Buffet Girl, James Lugton as Actor, Damien Strouthos as Lignière and Tim Walter as Actor. Sport For Jove's 2013 production of* Cyrano de Bergerac.
(Photos: Seiya Taguchi)

ACT ONE

TO THE MOON

A representation of the Hotel de Bourgogne theatre. A stage within the stage. A curtain. Footlights. The entrance, a large door or curtain, half open. A piano. Chandeliers.

A fusion of periods: between Rostand's own La Belle Époque and the coming outbreak of World War I (late 1913).

Characters arrive by degrees—specific timing is at the director's discretion. They are: VALVERT, DE GUICHE, *theatre punters* [TROOPERS, BURGHERS, LACKEYS, PAGES, MARQUISES, PATRONS, PICKPOCKET, STREET KID], *and theatre staff* [BELLEROSE, BUFFET GIRL, MUSICIANS].

Fluid pace once the stage begins to populate, building momentum right through to the opening of the 'play'.

VALVERT *and* DE GUICHE *enter.*

BELLEROSE: Hey, where's your money?
VALVERT: I get in free.
BELLEROSE: Why?
VALVERT: [*brushing him off, walking alone into the space*] Presidential Cavalry.
BELLEROSE: And you?
DE GUICHE: I don't pay.
BELLEROSE: Because?
DE GUICHE: I'm a musketeer!
BELLEROSE: Pardon, Commander de Guiche.

> *A* MARQUISE *arrives, overdressed, enormous picnic basket, copious alcohol.*

MARQUISE: [*seeing the seating already occupied*] Bugger me, you have to come early.
BELLEROSE: Ticket?
MARQUISE: Industry comp.

> *A* PICKPOCKET *and a* STREET KID *enter.*

PICKPOCKET: [*to the* KID] Right, my little orphan of Orpheus, pay attention: [*setting the rules*] wallets, purses, watches, anything— we steal from the rich and conceal from the poor. There's only one rule—we get caught, I never saw you before in my life. Right, let's go fishing.
VALVERT: [*to* BUFFET GIRL] A kiss; before the lights are lit!
BUFFET GIRL: Get off me.

> *He strengthens his grip. She sees the* KID *watching.*

He'll see!
VALVERT: [*taking in the* KID] He'll admire!
BUFFET GIRL: [*desperate now, seeing* DE GUICHE] What about your captain?
VALVERT: He's a colonel.

> *He kisses her forcefully.*

BELLEROSE: [*conducting the* STREET KID, *his pocket already picked*] Appalling. Sit here, son.

> *In this moment,* BELLEROSE *continues, with great nostalgia.*

To think, my boy, this is the theatre where they played Corneille, Molière.
STREET KID: And Voltaire!
BELLEROSE: And Racine!
DE GUICHE: What's the play?
BELLEROSE: *La Lune.* [*To the* STREET KID, *pointing*] I was up there, the first night of … *L'école des Ménages*—
DE GUICHE: [*shouting from the upper gallery*] Balzac!
BELLEROSE: And the actors … Bernhardt, La Beaupré, Jodelet! Montfleury!

> CHRISTIAN *appears with* LIGNIERE.

LIGNIERE: Sound like infectious diseases to me.
Well, my friend, I'd love to help you if I could,
But it's pretty clear your pretty dear … isn't coming!
And I know a bank where the wild times blow!
CHRISTIAN: No, stay, she'll come. A little longer, please.
Help me find a way to meet her.
LIGNIERE: You could try: 'Good evening, pleased to meet you,
My name is—'

ACT ONE

CHRISTIAN: I'm afraid. She may be one of these ...
LIGNIERE: Women?
CHRISTIAN: No; one of these ... clever ...
LIGNIERE: Women?
CHRISTIAN: One of these *coquettes, précieuses* ... *exquisites*—
LIGNIERE: Intellectuals?
CHRISTIAN: Intellectuals. The way they speak, and write, and ... speak, and talk. I'm terrified—I'm a soldier—
LIGNIERE: Christ, I'm terrified you're a soldier!
CHRISTIAN: No, I mean I'm a soldier—*fighting* is my line, not writing—
LIGNIERE: That's quite good.
CHRISTIAN: No, listen. I'm ... awkward ... this language they use—the way they talk—in conversation, in the gazettes, in letters—in conversation. This is Paris, not ... not where I come from.
LIGNIERE: Do you speak French?
CHRISTIAN: Yeah.
LIGNIERE: Do they speak French?
CHRISTIAN: Yeah.
LIGNIERE: Speak French.
CHRISTIAN: I'll die of shame. I'll show my ... lack of ... of ...
LIGNIERE: Wit? Brains? Confidence. Self-esteem. Poise. Nerve. Spirit?

    CHRISTIAN'*s body sags with defeat.*

Posture! Courage.
CHRISTIAN: No, courage I have.
LIGNIERE: Good. A drink I have not. I'm off.

    LE BRET *enters, unseen.*

CHRISTIAN: I don't even know her name.
LIGNIERE: Look, my flame waits for me, friend, at the tavern. You die of shame; I won't die of a thirst.
CHRISTIAN: [*in the pit*] Wait. Here comes the buffet girl [*pronouncing it 'buffette'*].
LIGNIERE: Buffet [*correcting him: 'buff ... ay'*].
CHRISTIAN: Buffet ...?
LIGNIERE: Buffet ... as in ballet.
CHRISTIAN: Oh, ball-et!
LIGNIERE: *Do* you speak French?

BUFFET GIRL: Orange juice?
LIGNIERE: No!
BUFFET GIRL: Milk?
LIGNIERE: Ooh.
BUFFET GIRL: Raspberry water?
LIGNIERE: God help me.
BUFFET GIRL: Bordeaux wine?
LIGNIERE: Here, I'll stay for a bit. [*To* BUFFET GIRL] That's fine.
ALL: Ragueneau!

> RAGUENEAU *enters, dressed in the Sunday clothes of a pastrychef, going quickly to* LIGNIERE.

LIGNIERE: Ragueneau! Poet, and prince of pastrycooks.
RAGUENEAU: Sir, have you seen Monsieur de Cyrano?
LIGNIERE: [*introducing him to* CHRISTIAN] Permit me. Ragueneau. Confectioner, actor, anthology of modern poetry, postmodern poetry, early modern poetry, late early modern poetry, middle-of-the-road poetry, a middling poet himself.
RAGUENEAU: [*well-accustomed to this warm satire*] Thank you.
LIGNIERE: *And* pastrychef to the stars. Born from a tart, and never looked back!
RAGUENEAU: You do me too great an honour ... Have you seen—?
LIGNIERE: [*not letting him off the hook, his famous selflessness*] Nay, he serves the starving and accepts only poetry in return! Admit it.
RAGUENEAU: [*humbly, crumbs falling at his feet*] Some writers come to my shop.
LIGNIERE: And you fill their bellies! On credit!
It's true—his generosity knows no sense!
For a little ode, he gives ...
RAGUENEAU: A little pie ...
LIGNIERE: And for a sonnet?
RAGUENEAU: A few buns!
LIGNIERE: [*severely*] Fourteen buns!
RAGUENEAU: A poet's dozen!
LIGNIERE: Cream buns at that.
CHRISTIAN: What would you give for a play?
RAGUENEAU: My life. My heart.
LIGNIERE: He likes the theatre.

RAGUENEAU: To distraction. [*Finally introducing himself properly*] Ragueneau.

A VOICE *shouts from the upper gallery:*

VOICE: Light it up!

The theatre starts to fill with light.

LIGNIERE: Baron de Neuvillette.
CHRISTIAN: Christian. Delighted to um … er …
LIGNIERE: The gentleman has come far, from the north, Touraine. His tongue should arrive shortly.
RAGUENEAU: Touraine, really?
LIGNIERE: A stranger to Paris.
CHRISTIAN: Well, I have been ten days in Paris; I join the Guards, tomorrow.
RAGUENEAU: Good fortune. [*To* LIGNIERE] You've not seen Cyrano?
LIGNIERE: No. How did you pay for your tickets, ha?—With cakes? Your seat, tonight, come on, just between us, what did it cost you?
RAGUENEAU: Four custards, fifteen puffs.
LIGNIERE: And the program?
RAGUENEAU: Forty cashews. He's really not here. He has to be here.
LIGNIERE: Why so?
RAGUENEAU: Montfleury is acting!
LIGNIERE: Ah, the tub of lard is acting, yes, three hundred pounds of pork will sweat and stumble through Racine … and … so …?
RAGUENEAU: Surely you've heard. Cyrano strictly forbade him to show his face on the stage for a full year.
LIGNIERE: [*inhaling his fourth glass*] And to quote myself … so …?
RAGUENEAU: [*handing the playbill*] Montfleury will play tonight!
MARQUISE: [*chiming in*] There is nothing he can do.
RAGUENEAU: Nothing? Well, something may come of nothing.
VALVERT: [*the conversation evolving into a public one*] Who or what is Cyrano?
PATRON: He's a soldier.
RAGUENEAU: A swordsman!
VALVERT: Well-born?
LIGNIERE: Well … born! … with a long sword.
RAGUENEAU: A poet.

LIGNIERE: Musician.
RAGUENEAU: Fighter.
LIGNIERE: Philosopher.
RAGUENEAU: Astronomer!
MARQUISE: And he tends to stand out in a crowd.
LE BRET: He's the most remarkable being under the moon.
LIGNIERE: Le Bret! Remarkable indeed. His face is an eyesore. Makes my eyes sore. The most anomalous face you ever saw.
CHRISTIAN: Why?
RAGUENEAU: It's ludicrous, extravagant, bizarre …
LE BRET: It's a masterpiece.
LIGNIERE: Well, it's a piece, no question. An olfactory double-helping.
RAGUENEAU An evolutionary apostrophe. He owes an apology to Darwin.
LIGNIERE: Or Darwin to him!
RAGUENEAU: [*drawing an audience*] He's whimsical, excessive, dazzling, wild;
He trails his sword like a barnyard cock.
Rodin would fail to carve his profile,
No quarry would yield him sufficient rock.
You see, my new friend, he carries a nose—

His playfulness dies, replaced with a certain sadness.

That—well—if only it could detach—
LE BRET: He'll keep it on. And God forbid you pay it mind.
VALVERT: [*interjecting proudly*] So he's a Gascony-proud and insolent jack.
LE BRET: To his friends, yes.
VALVERT: And to his enemies?
LE BRET: He's Cyrano de Bergerac.

Silence.

LIGNIERE: He's also not here.
RAGUENEAU: He will be! I'll wager a *poulet-à*-Ragueneau.

Murmurs of admiration in the hall.

ROXANE *appears in her box. She seats herself in front, the* DUENNA *at the back.*

CHRISTIAN: Now, tell me, quickly—who is she?

ACT ONE

LIGNIERE: [*between sips*] Ah—she's your flame? Well! Second name: Robin. Christened: Madeleine. Known, craved and feared—as Roxane.

CHRISTIAN: Feared?

LIGNIERE: Awed! She's unmarried. Refined. Artistic. Athletic. Agnostic. Cultivated. Captivated ... and ... literary.

CHRISTIAN: Literally what?

LIGNIERE: Literary. Bookish!

CHRISTIAN: Bookish?

LIGNIERE: She's-an-intellectual. Your-worst-nightmare.

CHRISTIAN: [*numb*] An intellectual?

LIGNIERE: Literally.

CHRISTIAN: I knew it.

At this moment DE GUICHE, *with white sash across his breast, enters the box, and stands talking intimately with* ROXANE.

[*Starting*] Who is that?

LIGNIERE: Aha! De Count de Guiche. He's in love—at her. But wedded, noosed as far as he's concerned, to the niece of the Cardinal. And if he can't have her no-one will. And by no-one, I mean our friend with the perm. M-hm. De Guiche would marry Roxane to Monsieur de Valvert, a viscount, a brilliant duellist but vacant viscount, with no idea how to handle such a prize. So—everyone's happy—Valvert hits puberty, and de Guiche hits the back staircase when Valvert travels on business—so he hopes.

CHRISTIAN: No!

LIGNIERE: Yes, he's done it before. Hitch the young hen to the complaisant cock and foul the nest while he's out counting his chickens.

CHRISTIAN: *No!*

LIGNIERE: Never fear, she'll none of the bargain; but de Guiche is powerful, and can persecute the daughter of a deceased untitled gentleman, can make her wish she'd never been hatched. Someone should write a song about it. Oh, that's right, I did. Exposed the whole dirty business, really hit him where it hurts.

CHRISTIAN: What did he do?

LIGNIERE: He hasn't done it yet. But he will. He always gets his man. Perhaps a reprise will jog his memory ...

Staggering to his piano, raising his glass, LIGNIERE *slams into a tune and readies to sing.*

CHRISTIAN: No, don't. Goodnight.
LIGNIERE: Where are you going?
CHRISTIAN: I'm going to duel the duellist!
LIGNIERE: No, you are going to listen …
CHRISTIAN: I've heard enough.
LIGNIERE: Stay where you are—
CHRISTIAN: *Why?*
LIGNIERE: Firstly, 'Christian de Serviette', he will kill you.
Secondly, bristle up your intellect, she is looking at you.
CHRISTIAN: She isn't? She is—isn't she? Is she still?
LIGNIERE: Still. Still. And yet still. As life itself.
CHRISTIAN: She is!
LIGNIERE: Isn't she just!

He stands, looking at her. The PICKPOCKET, *seeing him, head in air and open-mouthed, draws near.*

Well. Drink her in. I'll be drinking out.
I have an addiction and a reputation to uphold.

LIGNIERE *goes out, reeling.*

LE BRET, *who has been all around the hall, comes back to* RAGUENEAU, *reassured.*

LE BRET: Well, no sign of Cyrano. It's strange.
RAGUENEAU: I don't understand it.
LE BRET: One hope is left to me—that he hasn't seen the playbill!
MARQUISE: Begin! Let's get this show on the road.

VALVERT *has now joined* DE GUICHE.

DE GUICHE: Valvert. Will you come?

He heads toward the stage, followed by the MARQUISES *and* GENTLEMEN. *Turning, he calls—*VALVERT *is with* ROXANE, *engaging with her hand.*

Come, Valvert!

CHRISTIAN, *who is watching and listening, starts on hearing the name.*

CHRISTIAN: He's as good as dead. I'll hurl it in his face. My—
  Reaching for the glove in his belt/pocket, he finds the hand of the
  PICKPOCKET. *He turns around.*
Hey?
PICKPOCKET: Good house tonight! Practically in one another's pockets.
CHRISTIAN: [*holding him tightly*] So I see. I was looking for a glove.
PICKPOCKET: [*smiling piteously*] And you found a hand. Let me go—
  ow—and I'll tell you a secret.
CHRISTIAN: [*tightening on him*] A secret. What is it?
  Beat.
  Too late.
  CHRISTIAN *makes to strike him.*
PICKPOCKET: The drunk ... Lignière ... who just left you ...
CHRISTIAN: Well?
PICKPOCKET: He has an hour to live. Give or take.
  That song he wrote at a great man's expense;
  The great man has predictably taken offence
  And a hundred men are posted tonight ... to kill him.
CHRISTIAN: A hundred men! How do you know this?
PICKPOCKET: I'm one of them.
CHRISTIAN: Where are they posted?
PICKPOCKET: [*with great dignity*] Oh, etiquette please.
CHRISTIAN: What?
PICKPOCKET: Professional etiquette. Honour among thieves.
CHRISTIAN: And assassins?
PICKPOCKET: It's an economic imperative.
CHRISTIAN: [*tightening his grip*] Where are they posted?
PICKPOCKET: At the Porte de Nesle—it's on his way home—warn him.
CHRISTIAN: But where can I find him?
PICKPOCKET: Try the taverns—at this hour he'll be at The Grape and
  Grope—but try them all and leave a note.
CHRISTIAN: A hundred men against one drunk poet. Coward bastards.
  And to leave her just when I found her ... [*At* VALVERT] And him!
  [*Back to the* PICKPOCKET] You'll keep ... meanwhile ...
  He slaps him violently with the glove as a gage.
  ... keep this.

CHRISTIAN *hurries out.*
MARQUISE: Come on! Lights up! Begin!
A knock is heard upon the stage. Everyone is motionless. A pause.
DE GUICHE & OTHERS: Ssh!
Three knocks are heard on the stage. The curtain opens in the centre. Tableau. The MARQUISES, *in insolent attitudes, are seated on each side of the stage. The scene represents a levitating hot air balloon and moon/cosmos-scape—the balloon has ascended the atmosphere. Lustres light the stage; violins play softly.*
LE BRET: [*to* RAGUENEAU] Montfleury enters next?
RAGUENEAU: [*also in a low voice, checking the program*] Yup.
ALL: Sshh!
MONTFLEURY *enters to applause, falling to silence and stage action without speech. Enormously stout, he embodies the moon.*
RAGUENEAU: No, Cyrano. I've lost my wager.
LE BRET: Thank God.
ALL: Sshhh!
From within the balloon basket, high above the stage, JODELET *recites Paul Verlaine's poem, 'Le Soir'.*
JODELET: *La lune est rouge au brumeux horizon;*
Dans un brouillard qui danse, la prairie
S'endort fumeuse et la grenouille crie
Par les joncs verts ou circule un frisson.
Les fleurs des eaux referment leurs corolles;
Des peupliers défilent aux lointains
Droits et serrés, leurs spectres incertains;
Vers les buissons errent les lucioles;
Les chats-huants s'eveillent, et sans bruit
Rament l'air noir avec leurs ailes lourdes,
Et le zénith s'emplit de lueurs sourdes.
Blanche, Venus émerge, et c'est la nuit.
MONTFLEURY: [*after bowing low*] *La lune blanche*
Luit dans les bois;
L'étang reflète,

ACT ONE

Profond miroir,
La silhouette
Du saule noir
Où le vent pleure ...
Rêvons, c'est l'heure.
O Vénus, ô Déesse!

VOICE: [*almost disappointed, from somewhere in the hall*] You fat fool. I ordered you to stay away.

General stupor. Murmurs.

I thought I made it clear, that for a full year, you were not to appear.

LE BRET: Cyrano!

MONTFLEURY: But ...

VOICE: Is it your artistic pride? You could have told people you were resting. Or pregnant.

Mixed laughter and scorn for the interjections.

For the space of twelve new moons, you gross balloon, you were asked to take that weight off your feet. Do you defy me?

Various characters call out: 'Peace! Enough!'—'Let him be!'—'Play on, Montfleury—fear nothing!'

MONTFLEURY: [*in a trembling voice*] *La lune blanche*
    Luit dans les bois—

VOICE: [*more fiercely*] Get off!

MONTFLEURY: [*with resolve*] *L'étang reflète,*
    Profond miroir—

VOICE: Oh no! The fat ship sails on. So much cargo in his hold, so much fuel in his tanks, so many viewing decks, he doesn't see the iceberg!

Shock and distaste at the topicality of the joke—1913.

What? Too soon?

MONTFLEURY: [*trembling more and more*] *La silhouette—*

VOICE: Shall I make some portholes?

Various characters call out: 'Oh, come on!'—'You're a disgrace!'—'Ignore him, Montfleury!'—'He's all talk, Montfleury!'

MONTFLEURY: [*choking*] *Du saule noir*
    Où le vent pleure ...

CYRANO *appears suddenly in the pit, his beaver cocked fiercely, his moustache bristling, his nose terrible to see.*

CYRANO: Okay, Count von Landmark—get off. Offal. Off the boards, plank.

Sensation.

MONTFLEURY: [*to the management*] This is disgraceful.

JODELET: That's enough, monsieur, you are not welcome in this theatre.

General applause.

Continue, Montfleury.

CYRANO: Discontinue, Mount Fluid. Fat man, take warning!
[*Now with deadly intent*] Another word and I will slit you up.

LE BRET: You will not, Cyrano.

CYRANO: Out he goes!

Silence.

Is he gone yet?
[*Mounting the stage*] So be it!

MONTFLEURY: [*with simple dignity and sensing his audience's empathy— stopping* CYRANO *in his tracks*] You are a bully, sir—and as such, you are clearly the most frightened and vulnerable person in this room. You feel you have no self-worth so you divest others of theirs. Your mother's love perhaps was wanting.

Silence.

Deep applause from the pit—in the absence of theatre, they are now witnessing something better.

THEATRE STAFF / PUNTERS: Bravo! Well said, Montfleury!

CYRANO: My mother's love? I see. You may be right.
Perhaps I had problems breastfeeding ... do you think?

MONTFLEURY: No! *No!* Not at all.
But by insulting me, you insult the very muses.

CYRANO: The muses! Listen, Sigmund Fraud, the closest you have come to those nine fine Greek women is eating their moussaka.

Applause and laughter from the pit.

THEATRE STAFF / PUNTERS: Montfleury! Montfleury!

CYRANO: [*touching his scabbard*] Don't make me check my props.

ACT ONE

The circle around him widens. CYRANO *is furious that the lights have returned to performance state.*

[*To* MONTFLEURY] Last chance.

MARQUISE: [*from the darkness somewhere in the crowd*] Where's your authority?
We paid for a play,
You're the minority,
You go away.

Lights return (worker lights perhaps).

CYRANO: Who said that?

The CHORUS *draw back again.*

Let me but hear, once more, that childish rhyme,
And I'll slaughter every one of you.
Who was it?

Silence, stillness.

Then I challenge the whole pit collectively!
We'll make a list, here [*handing a book to a* PATRON] start taking names.
A surname is enough for a hero's epitaph.
Put up your hands or take a number.

Several arms begin to consider movement.

For those about to die, we salute you.
For those about to salute, I'll be killing you.
Who's first. You, sir? How about you? No! You? No?

Silence.

Not one hand?—Not one headstone? A finger? Good.

He returns to the stage, where MONTFLEURY *waits in agony.*

Where were we? Listen, Count von Zeppelin,
You floating haemorrhoid, I count to three,
Then I lance you.

MONTFLEURY: I ... er—

CYRANO: [*settling himself in the middle of the stage*] One!

He claps.

Untie the ropes, airship.

THEATRE STAFF / PUNTERS: [*amused, growing in excitement*] Ah!
MONTFLEURY: This is—
CYRANO: Two! Do you hear your cue—full moon? At the third clap—eclipse yourself.
MONTFLEURY: Under the circumstances, I—
CYRANO: Three!

    MONTFLEURY *disappears. Tempest of laughs, whistling cries, etc.*

THEATRE STAFF / PUNTERS: Coward ... come back!

    Delighted, CYRANO *sits back in his chair, arms crossed.*

CYRANO: Come back if you dare!
JODELET: Where is the theatre manager?

    BELLEROSE *comes forward and bows.*

THEATRE STAFF / PUNTERS: Ah! Here's Bellerose!
BELLEROSE: [*elegantly*] My noble friends ... the great tragedian whom you all love ...
Has left the building ...
THEATRE STAFF / PUNTERS: Coward! Come back, Montfleury!

    Some characters call out 'No!'; others 'Yes!'

JODELET: [*being extracted from her balloon aloft, to* CYRANO] Monsieur, why do you so hate our Montfleury?
CYRANO: [*still seated, graciously*] Good question. Two answers. Both conclusive.
First. He's a terrible actor. Think of a walrus doing cabaret. Verse that should dance like silk is dredged like mud and flung in vomitous fistfuls. He's the subtlety of a snowplough, he bludgeons pathos with a mallet. He has no integrity, character, or dimension—except horizontal. He treats the audience as a mirror. His only motivation is masturbation!

    Beat.

During intermission, he's fine.
DE GUICHE: The second reason?

    Beat.

CYRANO: Well, that's my secret.
BELLEROSE: And what about our box office? These people's money?

ACT ONE

CYRANO: [*leaving*] They got a show.

BELLEROSE: What about our takings?

CYRANO: Bellerose, that is the first intelligent word spoken this evening. I would not have Thespis go hungry. Where would the theatre be without funding?

He throws a bag on the stage.

THEATRE STAFF / PUNTERS: [*dazzled*] Oh!

BELLEROSE: [*weighing the purse*] Monsieur, feel free to close us down the same time tomorrow night.

The THEATRE STAFF *and* PUNTERS *boo, whistle, etc.*

Thank you, ladies and gentleman, please leave quietly and consider our neighbours.

The THEATRE STAFF *and* PUNTERS *begin to exit but get caught up in the next scene.*

LE BRET: [*to* CYRANO] Idiot.

CYRANO: Le Bret.

PATRON: [*a 'real' member of the contemporary audience with a young* CHILD] Excuse me, mate, unacceptable, we've been coming here for four years, we love these guys, and—

BELLEROSE: Just take a seat, sir.

PATRON: No, I won't take a seat—I paid for this seat— [*To* CYRANO] Who do you think you are …?

CYRANO: Well, if you were listening, I'm a playwright, philosopher, astronomer …

PATRON: Oh, you write plays yourself, do you?

CYRANO: I've been known to doodle.

PATRON Right, well yer motives are pretty transparent. You like attention, yeah? Instead of talent and respect. Do you know what I think you are, d'you know what my son thinks you are? A bore!

CYRANO: [*to* LE BRET] That's my second diagnosis today.

Making his way out, the PATRON *returns for a last word, taking out his phone.*

PATRON: Actually, who's your agent?

CYRANO: Nobody. [*To* LE BRET] He thinks I'm a bore.

PATRON: Nobody?—You don't have an agent?

CYRANO: No. Good evening.
CHILD: Let's go, Dad. He's got a sword.
PATRON: Let Dad handle this, mate, you're going to learn how to stand up for yourself. [*To* CYRANO] No agent to protect you, huh?
CYRANO: [*referring to his sword*] Oh, I always wear protection. [*To* LE BRET] Do you think I'm a bore?
PATRON: Well, theatregoers have long memories.
CYRANO: Mine's longer by three feet of steel.
PATRON: You threatening me, mate?
CYRANO: Not if you leave, off you go. Farewell.
Exit, pursued by a bore. Or tell me why you're staring at my nose.

The room stops.

PATRON: I ... er ... excuse me?
CYRANO: [*moving to him*] Does it astonish you? It imbalances the stage? It confuses you.
PATRON: Not at all.
CYRANO: It disturbs the equilibrium perhaps? Too much ying, a little too much—yang.
PATRON: No, I was very careful not to look.
CYRANO: Careful *not* to look? [*Aghast*] Why not look at it? Is there something wrong with it?
PATRON: No.
CYRANO: Then it disgusts you!
PATRON: No, sir.
CYRANO: It's too lurid perhaps? Too vivid?
PATRON: No, no, no.
CYRANO: Too present? Too—much—in the centre of my face?
PATRON: No, on the contrary! ... It's just exactly ... right in the centre of your face.
CYRANO: [*getting to the point*] Then perchance you think it ... large?
PATRON: Heavens no, it's small, it's ... minute, miniscule ...
CYRANO: [*to* LE BRET] Alright, that is clearly ridicule. Small—my nose? Small?
PATRON: God help me!
CYRANO: It's enormous! It's obscene, you flat-faced freak!—
My nose is the largest appendage in this room.

This thing is huge, it's my pride and joy.
You rob me of my very definition.
Who here knows not that the width, length and breadth
Of a man's nose, is in direct proportion—
JODELET: [*an involuntary outburst of excited apprehension*] Oh no—!
CYRANO: To his soul? It measures affability, virility,
Liberality, [*and to the* JODELET] and, yes, even reproductive speciality,

   JODELET *grips a chair.*

This ensures I'm well-endowed
With graces lost on faces such as yours.
I could eat off your face. It's like a plate,

   He examines the PATRON *closely.*

It's like the dead sea—with eyes—I can't find
A profile, a landmark to guess True North.
You're a void ...

   He slaps the PATRON.

And yet I find you with my hand.

   Hand on his hilts.

Unless you'd like a piercing for that mug,
Es-car-go! Enjoy Paris, you pug-nosed slug.
VALVERT: Sir—
This unarmed fool may say that thing is small,
I'm more content to call a spade a spade.

   Intense proximity.

That thing of yours—your nose—is big. It's—um—very big.
CYRANO: [*gravely*] Very!
VALVERT: [*laughing*] Ha!
CYRANO: [*imperturbably*] Is that it ...?
VALVERT: That—is that.
CYRANO: [*with deep and genuine disappointment, disarmingly frank*]
Oh, young man, that moment had such promise!
The entrance, the timing of the interjection.
Your voice gave you away; it made you flummox,
You need to breathe from here ...

He touches VALVERT*'s diaphragm.*

Feel that connection?

Opening the scene to the audience, on stage and off:
The things you could have said before this choir,
To belittle this eruption, this erection;
Oh, for a second chance, 'A muse of fire,
To ascend the brightest heaven of invention'.
Let me direct you; first, let's try—Aggressive:

VALVERT *fails to improvise.* CYRANO *does so in his place.*

'Fetch the guillotine! Let's amputate!'

Some shock and laughter among those spectating.

No, too much attack, too early; try—Impressive:
'Wow! The blood bank must be thrilled when you donate'.
Theatrical: 'A plague on both these houses …!'
Decorum: '*Please* put that back in your trousers'.

There is a growing enjoyment now at CYRANO*'s seemingly good-natured self-ridicule.*

Olympian: 'On'ya marks, get set— [*thrusting his head forward*] I never lose!'
Pythagoras: [*measuring his nose*] 'Bet the squares don't equal *that* hypotenuse …!'
Erotic: [*grabbing onto a chair in painful ecstasy*] 'Too much! Too much!'—'Why it's just the tip …'

A wowserish reaction from many. CYRANO *reacts to the condemnation.*

Oh, come on, you've all seen a stiff upper lip!

He's won them back.

Sightseeing: 'Ah, the pyramid of Giza—Jesus!—look at the pyramid on that geezer!'
A gift: 'For your coalmines … it's a canary'.
Aqualine: 'I'd love to see your Julius Caesar,
You could beware the Ides of March in February …'
Envious: 'Wish I could smoke in the rain!'
Bewilderment: 'You oughta see the grindstone …!'

Telegram for Mr Bergerac: 'Oh, *again* ...
Paris wants to excavate *more* limestone'.
Friendly: 'Usher—I'd like to buy this man a drink,
A *bloody* Mary. No, a *Looonnnggg* Island ice tea.'
Curious perhaps: 'What makes you blink?
Is it reflex or too much gravity?'
Then just plain Thoughtless: 'You'd look good in mink.
But use your nasal hair, you'll save a fortune.'
Or—Controversial: 'I suppose you think
A face like this will legalise abortion?'

> *A huge reaction from the crowd at the scandalous reference, so* CYRANO *has to reign it back in to less offensive material.*

Alright, apologies, apologies ...
A touch more Gracious: 'You must be fond of birds,
To give them such a vast and Gothic perch'.
Existential, or if you like, Absurd:
'We've found God! He has a portable church'.
Artistic: 'Your self-portrait ... is a landscape,
Isn't it?', or perhaps Geology:
'Is that a rock, a headland, or a cape?
Looks more like a *peninsula* to me!'

> *The* PICKPOCKET *calls out suddenly, boldly joining the mood.*

PICKPOCKET: Cartography!

> CYRANO *considers then goes with it:*

CYRANO: Cartogra—? Ohh yes: 'Hope that mountain's not to *scale* ...!'
CHILD: [*boldly*] Moby Dick!
CYRANO: [*slightly taken aback, approaching the* CHILD] Moby Dick?
You'd have me call myself a whale? Well ...

> *He picks the* CHILD *up by a scruff of clothing. The crowd jolts forward in fear of where this is going. Then suddenly* CYRANO *hoists the* CHILD *aloft, pulls a handkerchief from his pocket and bellows:*

'We've found her, Cap'm, *thar she blows*'!

> *Huge delight from the assembly as* CYRANO *blows hard into the handkerchief.*

Archeological: 'We also found the Grail!
'It was there the whole time, right under *his nose!*'
Desperate: 'Give up smoking, you can do it,
We've lost a dozen chimney sweeps this week,
It's Dickensian to put these children through it;
Close those Satanic Mills, it's just too bleak'.
Or …
Captain's Log, 'We're four miles from the peak!'
Surgical: [*sniffing*] 'Ah, I think we've lost a nurse …'
Emily Bronte: '*There's* some Heights to make you Wuther'.
Oedipal: 'This cold is like a curse,
Give me a tissue, wife'. 'What am I, ya mother?'
Commercial: 'A sign! … For a perfumery!'
Fiscal: 'Don't open both of those accounts'.
Biblical: 'When it bleeds, it's the Red Sea'.
Grateful: 'Well … I guess it's the snort that counts …'

> *He finds a newspaper on the piano.*

Ah, the classifieds: 'Warehouse available! Subdivided!'
Déjà vu: 'I've seen that nose before … No, I can't pick it …

> *Beat.*

I mean I really *can't pick it*!'
'Oh, I know you now … you're um … you're … Easter Island!'
Transport: 'On the Metro, do you buy two tickets?'
Typical actor: 'Bet the acoustics up there are *fantastic*'.
[*A sudden sneeze*] *Aachoo!*—'Hayfever! Get a beaver! We'll build a dam!'
Costume party: 'Okay, that mask is a little drastic …'
René Descartes: [*with a big sniff at* VALVERT] 'You stink, therefore I am …'

> VALVERT *swings a first hit at* CYRANO, *he's had it now.* CYRANO *effortlessly ducks and weaves, carrying on.*

St Nicholas!—'Easy one, come on … piece of cake …

> VALVERT*'s got nothing. The others join in a large chorus.*

'He sees you when you're sleeping, he *no … se* when *you're* awake!'
Anthropological: 'It's just a myth;

ACT ONE

An illusion made with mirrors; it's a stunt,
National Geographic said it was
The Hippocampocamelelephunt'.
Postmodern: '... nose ...'
Punctual: 'You're early! No ... you're late!'
Really turning on himself now:
Botanical: 'Do you stop and scare the roses?
And how'd you grow that moustache in the shade?'
Wisdom: 'Have you ever heard the saying,
"Don't cut off your nose to spite your face?"
Well, some maxims are not worth the obeying,
Just *cut it off*! It's not spite in your case!'
Paranoid: 'Can you smell what I'm thinking?'
A Pun!: 'That tower is an *eye-full* ... what a feat!'
Forecast: 'Either he sneezed or it's sprinkling'.
Romantic: 'That nose by any other name ...
  The whole crowd, invited by CYRANO, *joins for the answer:*
  '... would smell as sweet'.

  Applause from the delirious onlookers, oblivious to the mounting darkness of CYRANO's *self-ridicule. It has cost him a great deal, this self-harm, there will be a consequence for someone—only* DE GUICHE *is cognisant of it.*

Shall I go on or have you got The Point?
I skipped Pastoral-Historical, but felt
That Tragical could never disappoint:
'O that this too too ... solid flesh ... would melt'.
That's the sort of thing you might have said,
Had you had even a modicum of wit
In that vacuous unlettered feathered head,
But ... I'd never let you get away with it!
DE GUICHE: [*apprehensive*] Come away, Viscount. Leave it now.
VALVERT: [*desperate*] Such arrogance. Ha. Doesn't even wear gloves.
  A clown. Look at him.
CYRANO: [*deeply personal now*] I carry my adornments on my soul.
  Don't think I don't care how people see me.
  I never leave the house until I'm sure

I smell of immaculate liberty,
And polished independence. No manicured hands,
But I give my scruples the once-over.
True though. I wear no gloves, you got me there,
I have this one, left over from a pair,

> *A pathetic war-torn glove is produced.*

A lonely thing, its brother I can't trace,
I must have left it in some viscount's face.

> *He belts* VALVERT *with it, viciously.*

VALVERT: [*searching through rage*] Filthy, insolent, flat-footed, vagrant sack!

CYRANO: [*extending his hand or bowing deeply*] Cyrano-Savinien-Hercule de Bergerac.

> *With his glove,* VALVERT *returns the favour, leisurely, to* CYRANO*'s nose.*

DE GUICHE: Viscount de Valvert, come. That's an order.

CYRANO: [*suddenly, with convincing agony*] Agh … good God … oh … I'm sorry.

VALVERT: What is this? What's wrong with him?

CYRANO: [*through sharp suffering*] It's a twinge. It goes to sleep. It stiffens up.
It comes with letting it lie here in the damp.
If it gets no exercise it starts to throb.
Oh, God …

VALVERT: What does?

> *Recovered,* CYRANO *flashes his sword at the ready.*

CYRANO: My sword. It's got a cramp.

VALVERT: So be it!

> CYRANO *looks to* DE GUICHE—*a test of military law in a civil environment. Will he permit a duel?* DE GUICHE *turns and sits.*

Come, poet.

CYRANO: Actually I do get terribly bored while fighting. Pardon my prose, but would you be offended if I took this opportunity to compose?

ACT ONE

VALVERT: Compose?
CYRANO: Before you decompose.
I'd like to write a ballad of our duel.
Not after—but during—
[*To the crowd*] Is that too cruel?
An ode of strictest classical design,
And then to kill you—on the final line.
VALVERT: A ballad?
CYRANO: Not if you object—at your discretion!
Sorry to baffle with technical expression.
I'll explain:
Eight-line stanzas,
One quatrain,
And a coda,
Little splash of soda.
VALVERT: [*lunging dangerously*] Let's get on with it.
CYRANO: 'The day de Bergerac did a Parisian turd'.
VALVERT: What's that?
CYRANO: That's the title. You're the turd.

    VALVERT *makes another assault,* CYRANO *effortlessly avoids.*

Hold up, can you please remove your doublet?
[*Removing his own*] I need some flesh to score the final couplet.

    CYRANO *counts on his fingers.*

VALVERT: What is this?
CYRANO: Just choosing my rhymes.
VALVERT: Prat!
CYRANO: Good one—prat, hat, rat, tat.
Set?

He flies into it.

Suiting action to the words throughout the following fight, wild, exuberant reactions of hilarity grow to quiet horror.

    I thrust, then lightly throw my hat
    A pause, a languid storm at rest—
    Then chaos as I spy the rat,
    It thunders, and his throat's caressed …

Too early yet to end the prat
Let's work the floor, explore the space
It's blow for blow, it's tit for tat
But when the poem ends, that's that.

To take him heart? Or through the thigh?
Is that his groin you're pointing at?
Where shall I sting this butterly,
This feckless fond aristocrat?
Ooh, that was close, a note to self;
He's sharp on Passe-Avant Attaque
Don't underestimate his stealth,
But when the poem ends, that's that.

VALVERT: Shut up. *Shut your mouth!*

He spits in CYRANO*'s face.*

CYRANO: His temper stirs. His mouth is dry.
He wasted fluid when he spat.
He's ashen pale like winter sky
Let's take some blood.

CYRANO *cuts him.* VALVERT *cries out.*

It's just a pat.

Don't panic, boy, we're almost home.
Take a thought for family,
For mother, father, sister, comb
Through all you've ever wondered at.

He knocks VALVERT *to the floor—he's frightened like a child, this is very real now.*

Now stand! And face eternity.
This stage has bled for others too,
For Hamlets, Caesars. Hark!

VALVERT: What's that?
CYRANO: Your cue. I'm sorry.

CYRANO *kills him very suddenly.*

That—is that.

Silent awe and confusion.

ACT ONE

DE GUICHE *now controls the room and its consequences, of which even* CYRANO *is aware. Will he arrest him?*

DE GUICHE *stands and approaches* CYRANO, *returns his frail glove, orders the body to be removed, and leaves. All the others follow, except* RAGUENEAU, LE BRET *who has been at the body of* VALVERT, *and the* BUFFET GIRL. *They stare at the body. At some point* MONTFLEURY, *dressed in civvies, almost unrecognised in simple dignity, leaves.*

BELLEROSE: [*simply*] You can leave those lights. We rehearse after supper for tomorrow's farce.

    BELLEROSE *exits.*

RAGUENEAU: Will you to supper?
CYRANO: No.
LE BRET: Why not?
CYRANO: Because—
    Because I'm not as wealthy as I was.
LE BRET: Don't tell me that that purse was all you had.
CYRANO: It was indeed.
RAGUENEAU: Oh, *Cyrano*! … you're mad.

    RAGUENEAU *leaves, in some shock.*

LE BRET: What a fool!
CYRANO: But what a gesture!
BUFFET GIRL: Pardon me, sir. I couldn't help but hear.
    You mustn't starve. Take something. Please.
CYRANO: My dear,
    My Gascon pride forbids me to, I fear.

    LE BRET *despairs at his idiocy.*

But rather than upset my colleague here,
I'll not reject your kindness—just a mere—
Morsel—I'll take—
Oh, not very much—
Just a grape—
Only one.
A glass of water.
And half a macaroon.

Gravely, he carefully returns the other half.

LE BRET: You stubborn fool, you cannot live like this.

BUFFET GIRL: Nothing more, sir?

CYRANO: Yes ... your hand to kiss.

He kisses her hand with great humility and respect. She is profoundly moved.

BUFFET GIRL: Thank you, sir. Goodnight.

CYRANO: [*to* LE BRET] Right, you talk—I'll listen.

He stands at the buffet, and digests the grape.

Dinner ...!

Then the glass of water.

Wine ...!

Then the macaroon.

Dessert ...!
Ah! I was hungry.
You were saying?

LE BRET: Why must you make such enemies?

CYRANO: How many d'you think I made tonight?

LE BRET: Oh, forty, fifty, not counting the ladies.

CYRANO: Count! List them!

LE BRET: Well, Montfleury, the bourgeoisie, de Guiche,
This viscount's family, the playwright, the Academy ...

CYRANO: I have been busy!

LE BRET: Yes, but where does it lead you, in the end?
Is there a plan, because—

CYRANO: I've had too many plans, Le Bret, too many paths.
Now I've chosen one.

LE BRET: And which is that?

CYRANO: I've decided to excel at everything.

LE BRET: [*shrugging it off*] Ah. Very good.
So at the risk of provoking more nonsense, and notwithstanding our dead friend, why this spectacle tonight, this show of hate for Montfleury?

CYRANO: [*exploding*] That earthworm!
That fat paunch with a frog's face; that farce,

ACT ONE

That barely knows his belly from his arse,
Still deems himself a catch—a spur to women,
Goggle-eyed and strutting like God's given
Him a license to disgust with veiled lust,
I hate him—because—who wouldn't, I simply must.
I hate him since the day he dared to smile …
Upon … a girl, a friend, her, on the aisle …
I see it in my dreams, his filthy shows
Of love … a snail slithering on a … rose …

LE BRET: [*stupefied*] What? You're not? You are! Is it possible?

CYRANO: For me to love? … What? Too improbable?
[*Changing his tone, gravely*] I'm in love.

LE BRET: You never said …

CYRANO: You never asked.

LE BRET: This is wonderful.

CYRANO: Wonderful—look at me!
My shame precedes me everywhere I go.
What lover then could not this face embarrass?
And of course I love—inevitably—who?
The most beautiful woman in …

LE BRET: Paris.

CYRANO: The world.

LE BRET: No! You don't mean …?

CYRANO: He who has seen her smile has known perfection,
Instilling into trifles grace's essence,
Divinity in every careless gesture—
God, listen to me! I'm like an adolescent!

LE BRET: So—all is clear.

CYRANO: As teargas.

LE BRET: Your cousin, Madeleine Robin?

CYRANO: Roxane!

LE BRET: Well, tell her so! She already adores you.
She saw your double triumph here tonight!

CYRANO: One time I thought I would—before the wars, you
Remember—we were children. I was eight.
Even then I was under no illusions,
I knew I was as ugly as a bear,

But—the sea, the scent, the sky—it breeds confusion;
She was standing in the water—and her hair—
I took a breath— [*self-mocking*] a big breath—thought I'd die—
And asked if she would walk with me to school,
She turned—and I was gone, I ran—
LE BRET But *why*?
CYRANO: I saw my own reflection in the pool.
LE BRET: [*tenderly*] My friend! …
CYRANO: Why does providence allot such grace to some and makes others … *'The fixed figure for the time of scorn to point his slow unmoving finger at'?*
LE BRET: Are you crying?
CYRANO: No, never! I'm quoting! No tear deserves
So long a marathon to find the earth,
No! Tears are sublime—salted pearls of glass—
This nose makes the sublime ridiculous.
LE BRET: [*lashing out*] You're ridiculous. Give her more credit,
Give love more credit than just the slave of looks.
This girl that brought you food just now, you idiot,
She was entranced—not by the cover—by the book!
CYRANO: [*impressed*] Mmm, she was a little—taken—wasn't she?

They share a laugh. Then silence.

LE BRET: I saw her face—Roxane's—while you were fighting.
She was pale.
CYRANO: She was pale? Is that true?
LE BRET: As when a woman's heart is struck by lightning,
At the thought of losing …
CYRANO: What?
LE BRET: Losing you!

BELLEROSE *enters, conducting the* DUENNA.

BELLEROSE: Monsieur, a lady to see you …

Expectation blooms—the DUENNA *looms.*

CYRANO: Roxane's Duenna. Good evening, madame.
DUENNA: I have a message. From my mistress.
I'll come no closer in case you stab me.
CYRANO: Forgive me, madame … the stage stirs my blood!

ACT ONE

DUENNA: Then try the racetrack.
Someone wants to know where one could meet,
One's 'valiant' cousin—keeping it discreet.
CYRANO: Me—her cousin? Meet?
DUENNA: There are certain things one would like to say.
CYRANO: Certain ...
DUENNA: Things.
CYRANO: Things?
DUENNA: Is there an echo? Things! Private matters!
CYRANO: My God ...
DUENNA: Matters of feeling.
CYRANO: My God.
DUENNA: One goes to dawn mass tomorrow at Saint-Roch.
CYRANO: My God.
DUENNA: Yes, her God too. Is there somewhere private afterwards to meet?
CYRANO: Yes! ... Ah ... one wants to meet ... I'm thinking ... of where. *Mon dieu!* Ah ...
DUENNA: Yes?
CYRANO: *Mon dieu!* Ah, in the Rue—my God—Ragueneau's—the pastry shop—Rue de Théâtre!
DUENNA: Ragueneau's. Seven a.m. One will be there.
CYRANO: So will the other ... one ...
DUENNA: [*warning him*] And so will I!

    The DUENNA *exits.*

CYRANO: [*overwhelmed*] See me? A rendezvous?
LE BRET: [*some bitterness*] Call it a tryst.
You happy now?
CYRANO: [*falling into* LE BRET*'s arms*] She remembers I exist!
LE BRET: Are you *happy* now?

    No response.

At least becalmed!
CYRANO: Be calmed!? I'll be volcanic—burn the world!
I have ten hearts to share and twenty arms,
I'll take all Europe with my flag unfurled!

    The ACTORS *angrily reappear from backstage.*

ACTOR: [*entirely frank*] Excuse me there! We're rehearsing a new season, at reasonably short notice you'll recall. Do you mind if we 're-take' the theatre, unless you'd like to play our parts and all.

CYRANO: I would, I will, I can—I am a chorus;
A thousand men of Thebes; [*selecting one of the* ACTORS] I can be you!
I can be me, I can be ... [*taking a skull from one of them*] or not be, I am the walrus!
My God, please let me play the lion too!

LE BRET: I'm terribly sorry. Thank you. We'll be off ...

> LIGNIERE, *very drunk, very desperate, bursts back into the theatre, accidentally donning an ironical costume held by the* ACTORS. *The moment has the spontaneous theatricality of tragi-comedy.*

Lignière, what is it?

LIGNIERE: Help ... I got this note.
A hundred men ... don't like a song I wrote ...
I can't go home ... you hear ...

CYRANO: A hundred men ...?

LIGNIERE: The Port de Nesle ... all armed, the lot o'them ...
I can't go home ... Please ... let me stay with you ...

CYRANO: A *hundred* men ...

LIGNIERE: I know ...

CYRANO: No, it's too few!

> *Sword drawn,* CYRANO *makes to leave.*

LE BRET: De Berg—*You cannot fight a hundred men!*

> CYRANO *stops.*

CYRANO: Then this man will say that he had once a friend.

> CYRANO *sets off.*

LE BRET: [*stripping the drinking vessel from* LIGNIERE*'s lips*] Why die for one that cares not for himself?

CYRANO: I can't approve what this does for his health,

> *He is beginning to engage the whole group of* ACTORS.

But this man, this sponge, this sieve, this plastered relic,
Once did a thing I can but call angelic.

ACT ONE

Now, he can't bear water, to touch nor taste,
A liquid thing not corked, to him's a waste;
But, once, he saw a beauty—you remember—
Bathe her hands in holy water—
LIGNIERE: It was December—
CYRANO: It was December, nineteen-hundred'n'three—
Hear how this sot began the century!

Hugely significant and suspense-filled:

When that lady left the font—
JODELET: I am going to cry—
CYRANO: He kneeled before that well—and drank it dry!

Beat.

LE BRET: [*sarcasm, drenched with exhaustion at* CYRANO'*s esteem for futile gestures of romanticism*] Oh, well then, yes, of course, go make your stand.
And what about the bakery with Rox ... your cousin?
CYRANO: I'll head home once I've maimed a baker's dozen.
MARQUISE: Why one poor poet against a hundred men?
CYRANO: You can come, but I won't have you muscle in.

Great excitement and the gathering of items etc.

No aid nor warnings once the fun begins.
Strike up a fanfare on those violins.
Myself, my plume, my soul, 'it is the cause',
Fall in behind me. Stand. Porter. The doors.
LE BRET: [*to the* PATRON'S CHILD, *who has stayed throughout*] Your father was right, he is a bore.

A general gasp at the view of Paris—reflected in light upon the ACTORS'*faces.*

CYRANO: [*personal, barely audible*] Paris—nocturnal dreaming in the mist,
How you will long tomorrow for what you've missed.
A shudder of blood on bone on steel—a kiss
Echoed through sleeping streets, to beds in bliss.
The only auditor, voyeur—the moon,
One candle lights this whole proscenium,

Below, costumed in fog, a silver skein,
A moist and magic serpent, breathes the Seine,
Dumb witness to this myth and mystery,
Well—it will see tonight what it will see!

> *They all set off but* CYRANO *holds them momentarily, calling the* MARQUISE *to his shoulder.*

Mademoiselle asks why a hundred men
Seek to punish one poor poet's song,
Paris has known the answer all along,
Because he's a friend of mine.

ALL BUT LE BRET: To the Port de Nesle.

> CYRANO *exits, pursued by the* ACTORS. *Curtain.*

END OF ACT ONE

ACT TWO

PATRON OF THE TARTS

Ragueneau's cook and pastry shop in the grey dawn. A large, bustling kitchen/store at the corner of the Rue du Théâtre and the Rue de l'Arbre Sec, somewhat worse for wear but bursting at the seams with the creativity of Ragueneau's produce. Tables laden with rolls and dishes of food, some of them works of culinary art. Other tables surrounded with chairs/benches ready for consumers.

A small table in a corner is covered with papers, at which RAGUENEAU *is seated, sleeping amidst his writings.*

FIRST PASTRYCOOK *enters, carrying an elaborate fancy dish.*

FIRST PASTRYCOOK: Fruits in nougat!

    SECOND PASTRYCOOK *enters, carrying another dish.*

SECOND PASTRYCOOK: Custard!

    THIRD PASTRYCOOK *enters, carrying a roast, decorated with feathers.*

THIRD PASTRYCOOK: Peacock!

    FOURTH PASTRYCOOK *enters, carrying a batch of cakes on a slab.*

FOURTH PASTRYCOOK: Tarts!

    Entering, LISE *throws a basin of water over her sleeping/writing husband.*

LISE: Time to cook, not be a patron of the arts!

RAGUENEAU: [*raising his head—frank and despondent, oppressed*] Ah, the dawn—that burns the dreams of hopeful men.
Takes us from inks and rhymes to sinks and grime and then,
Puts copper pans and flans in hands that could be writing.
Tomorrow's ballads tossed in salads—how inviting!

    He rises.

[*To a* PASTRYCOOK] You—make that sauce longer, it's too short!

FIRST PASTRYCOOK: How much too short?
RAGUENEAU: [*tasting*] Three beats.
  [*To* SECOND PASTRYCOOK, *showing them some loaves*] This clef is misplaced; balance the metaphor.
  [*To* THIRD PASTRYCOOK, *showing them an unfinished pastry*] Put the comma here and see the difference?
  [*To* FOURTH PASTRYCOOK] The caesura comes between the hemistichs!
  [*To* LISE] Beautiful, isn't it?
LISE: Ridiculous.

  She puts a pile of papers on the counter.

RAGUENEAU: Paper bags! Good. Thank you.
  My God—woman—what have you done? This is poetry.
  These are the poems of my friends! Torn, dismembered,
  To make biscuit bags. These are manuscripts!
LISE: This indulgent crap was all we ever got
  As payment from that good-for-nothing lot.
  Why shouldn't I make use of it?
RAGUENEAU: By turning poetry to paper bags?!
LISE: [*moving off to the kitchen*] Yes—and profit.
RAGUENEAU: [*screaming after her*] My God! What would you do with prose?!

  As LISE *exits into the kitchen, she holds up a toilet roll made from his latest short story.*

CYRANO: [*bursting in, rapid pace to the exchanges*] What time is it?
RAGUENEAU: Six o'clock.
CYRANO: One hour.
RAGUENEAU: I neglected to pay your dues last night? Bravo!
CYRANO: For what?
RAGUENEAU: The fight.
CYRANO: Which one?
RAGUENEAU: The duel in verse!
LISE: [*returning*] I'm afraid that he can talk of nothing else!
CYRANO: Oh, that. I thought you were appalled.
RAGUENEAU: I abhorred the violence but … adored the rhymes.
LISE: [*crossing through*] Yes, heavens, don't do the crime if you can't do the rhyme!

RAGUENEAU: [*making passes with a utensil*] 'At the poem's end, that's that'!
[*With increasing enthusiasm*] 'At the poem's end—'
CYRANO: The time?
RAGUENEAU: Thirty seconds past six … [*One last thrust*] 'That's that'.
LISE: What's wrong with your hand?
CYRANO: Nothing, a scratch.
RAGUENEAU: What's happened? Are you in trouble?
CYRANO: It's nothing?
LISE: Are you telling the truth?
CYRANO: [*referencing the obvious*] Well, it must be one hell of a lie! Listen, I have an appointment, here at seven? What time now?
RAGUENEAU: *Forty* seconds past six. Are you in danger?
CYRANO: Possibly. I hope! Leave us alone, when the moment comes—
RAGUENEAU: I can't, my poets are due—
LISE: For their first meal of the day!
CYRANO: Disturb us for nothing, not the crack of doom. Understood? What time is it?
RAGUENEAU: Are you kidding? Same time, add ten seconds.
CYRANO: Please … when she comes … don't be here.
RAGUENEAU: [*pointing to the counter*] I'll just be there.
CYRANO: Don't be anywhere! A pen! … A pencil!
RAGUENEAU: [*giving him the one from behind his ear*] Here. Six-o-one.
CYRANO: What time is it? Thank you.

    A MUSKETEER, *with fierce moustache, enters.*

MUSKETEER: [*in a stentorian voice*] *Bonjour*—my good madame, my good monsieur.

    LISE *goes up to him quickly.*

CYRANO: [*turning around, watching the nature of their embrace*] Who's that?
RAGUENEAU: [*ashamed, embarrassed, resigned*] Oh—he's a friend—of my wife's.
CYRANO: Right. [*To himself*] Right. Now write. Fold. Give it to her. Change my life.

    He throws down the pen.

Coward—she wants to speak. You only need to say three words. [*To* RAGUENEAU] What time is it?

LISE, passing by, takes the enormous French clock from the wall and places it on his table.

Thank you. Why say a single word when I can write a thousand?

He is unable to begin.

Come on!
This letter I have written on my heart,
Torn it, burned it, written it again.
Now all I have to do is make a start.
No pressure. My whole future's in this pen.

He writes. Through the glass of the door the silhouettes of figures move uncertainly, faux hesitation. They are the four POETS, *dressed in black, conspicuously untidy, self-consciously bohemian, unwashed.*

LISE: Oh, here they come! The hungry and the poor.
  Husband—your friends, the freeloaders—at the door.
FIRST POET: [*entering, to* RAGUENEAU] *Confrère!*
SECOND POET: [*to* RAGUENEAU, *shaking his hands*] *Cher confrère!*
THIRD POET: Brother in art, Lord of the roast!
FIRST POET: Apollo of the *poulet*!

He sniffs, they all sniff, a ritual.

I love the smell of fruit flan in the morning.

The POETS *surround and embrace* RAGUENEAU.

RAGUENEAU: My boys, my friends, my lads, my hearts of gold.
FOURTH POET: Sorry we're late. We were stayed by the mob; you seen the crowd at the Porte de Nesle?
THIRD POET: Dead men everywhere, mercenaries, fugitives.
FIRST POET: Slashed head to tail.
SECOND POET: Carcasses. I counted eight.
CYRANO: [*with only passing interest*] Eight? I made it seven.
RAGUENEAU: [*to* CYRANO] You know about this, Cyrano? Were you there?
CYRANO: [*carelessly*] No, just passing through.

ACT TWO

FIRST POET: The old woman, on the corner, she says one man … one man!
THIRD POET: One man drove off ninety, butchered eight.
LISE: [*to the* MUSKETEER] Were you there?
MUSKETEER: [*touching his moustache*] Maybe!

>CYRANO, *writing a little way off, is heard murmuring from time to time.*

CYRANO: [*murmuring*] 'Je vous aime …'
SECOND POET: Blood, bone, their brains.
CYRANO: [*writing*] '… your lips, your eyes …'
RAGUENEAU: What?
CYRANO: Shh. '… vos yeux.'
FOURTH POET: [*filching a cake*] Right, down to it! My muse is famished!

>*The* POETS *help themselves.*

What have you written lately, Ragueneau?
RAGUENEAU: Oh, not much. A recipe in verse.
FIRST POET: [*eating, not listening*] We're listening.
RAGUENEAU: 'A Pugilist's Almanac to the Almond Tart'.
SECOND POET: The almond tart!
THIRD POET: I think I saw her last night in Pigalle.

>*Laughter, they eat on.*

RAGUENEAU: Poised on steady legs,
>First, beat your eggs
>A dozen blows, until it mercy begs.

>Then light and quick,
>Add lemon, froth it thick,
>Sting it from the ring and try a lick.

>When consistency's like silk,
>Left jab the milk,
>A right hand for the almonds and their ilk.

>Now upper cut the paste
>Watch any waste,
>Too close to the nuts you spoil the taste.

Push it to the edges,
The pastry wedges
Need a pounding then leave them out on ledges.

Once you've got it in the clinch,
Just add a pinch
Of ginger. Bake till countdown. It's a cinch!

They go on eating. Finally, the silence reminds them to applaud.
CYRANO *watches.*

CYRANO: A captive audience. Do you see how your voice lulls them into stuffing themselves?
RAGUENEAU: Yes, I see well enough, but I never look.
I need them, so I feed them.
They need to eat. I get a treat.
CYRANO: And what's that—more debt and a heart condition?
RAGUENEAU: No … just company, somebody to listen.
CYRANO: [*clapping him on the shoulder*] You're a good man, Ragueneau.

He watches as RAGUENEAU *goes after his friends.*

[*Sharply*] Lise! A word?

LISE *is talking tenderly to the* MUSKETEER. *She moves aside with* CYRANO.

So, this captain, this 'musketeer' … he laying siege to you?
LISE: Excuse me!
CYRANO: Is he battering at your gates?
LISE: I can defend my own portcullis, thank you. One look from these eyes is enough to quell his forces …

She focusses on CYRANO.

And any other's.
CYRANO: These blue conquerors look well conquered to me. I can see the whites of their flags.
LISE: How dare you …
CYRANO: I like Ragueneau, he's a friend of mine. Generous, yes, foolish, certainly … humiliated? Never.

He moves to the MUSKETEER.

A word to the wise … this castle's closed.

ACT TWO

The MUSKETEER *makes no response.*

LISE: [*to the* MUSKETEER] Are you going to swallow that? Say something. Slap him on the nose.

MUSKETEER: On the nose? ... Yes, yes I will. Later.

    LISE *exits, furious.*

CYRANO: [*from the doorway, signing to* RAGUENEAU *to draw the* POETS *away*] Ragueneau. Move.

RAGUENEAU: [*showing them the way to the kitchen*] Gentlemen, let's try some of that tart. Follow me.

FIRST POET: I thought you'd never ask.

    They all follow RAGUENEAU *in procession, after sweeping all the cakes off the trays.*

CYRANO: [*suddenly struck with superstition*] Faintest glimmer of hope—out comes the letter! No, no. If she closes the door with her left hand ... she loves me ... I give her the letter. No, the right hand.

    ROXANE *is now visible through the window or doorway.*

Left. Left! No, if she leaves her parasol up, if she leaves it open, she will be mine.

    ROXANE *and her* DUENNA *come in. She slams the door with her left hand into the parasol, almost breaking it, tries to close it, can't, so throws it into a waste barrel beside the table. The door remains open—*CYRANO *is none the wiser.*

[*Moving to remove the* DUENNA] Four words with you, madame?

DUENNA: If they are 'Please take a seat', that's fine.

    She sits centre.

CYRANO: Do you like eating?

DUENNA: I eat until I'm sick.

    CYRANO *catches up some of the paper bags from the counter.*

    RAGUENEAU *comes to the door and watches in some agony as the poems are employed as bags.*

CYRANO: Good. Here's a sonnet.

DUENNA: Oh.

CYRANO: In which we're going to stick—cakes!
DUENNA: Ah!
CYRANO: Would a meringue make an impression?
DUENNA: Sir, they're an obsession! I'll take cream, then go to confession.
CYRANO: Excellent. They'll be right at home here with Shelley.
As for this epic to a love-sick soul,
I think it's deep enough for a whole jam roll.

> RAGUENEAU *has now returned to the counter in some dismay.*

DUENNA: [*overwhelmed with expectation now*] You are a treasure!
CYRANO: That's a pleasure.
DUENNA: [*snatching a last treat*] And just a bun!
CYRANO: In the sun. Don't come back till you're done.

> *Shepherding her out the door briskly,* CYRANO *returns to find* ROXANE *now lost in the cake selection and* RAGUENEAU *back at his counter—it's not going well so far.*

ROXANE: What are these?
RAGUENEAU: Choc-éclair-cream puffs with cinnamon drizzle.
ROXANE: You had me at éclair—now you're trying to kill me!

> *All share a laugh.*

Three please. And those exquisite paper bags.
RAGUENEAU: [*distressed*] Ah, of course. And—ah—you'd like them wrapped?
ROXANE: Separately please. Thank you. I'm coming, sorry!

> ROXANE *smiles at* CYRANO. RAGUENEAU *takes a bag, and just as he is about to put in the puffs, he reads.*

RAGUENEAU: [*reading*] 'Ulysses thus, on leaving fair Penelope ...'
You really want them wrapped?
ROXANE: Enveloped!
RAGUENEAU: Ozymandius—not that one!
[*Reading*] 'Rose-cheeked Adonis hied him to the chase ...'
Oh, not Shakespeare, no ...
ROXANE: Oh yes, I love that one.

> *Taking the puffs and wrappers and moving to* CYRANO, *she quotes, ravishing the poem from memory. Hearing only of her looks thus far, we immediately meet her staggering mind, confidence, cultivation,*

fierce intelligence, sensuality—an astonishing introduction to why CYRANO *idolises her. She is effortlessly brilliant—reeling the poem off while eating.*

> Even as the sun with purple-colour'd face
> Had ta'en his last leave of the weeping morn,

She pulls window curtains to, to conceal her secret meeting.

> Rose-cheeked Adonis hied him to the chase,
> Hunting he loved, but love he laugh'd to scorn.
> Sick-thoughted Venus makes amain unto him,
> And like a bold-fac'd suitor, 'gins to woo him.

She sits on his lap with all the playfulness of a long and deep history of complete trust and friendship, immediately washing away whatever passage of time since they last spoke—she is playing Venus, characterising CYRANO *as Adonis—at times feeding him an éclair and eating herself.*

> Vouchsafe, thou wonder, to alight thy steed,
> And rein his proud head to the saddle-bow;
> If thou wilt deign this favour, for thy meed
> A thousand honey secrets shalt thou know:
> Here come and sit, where never serpent hisses,
> And being set, I'll smother thee with kisses;
>
> He burns with bashful shame: she with her tears
> Doth quench the maiden burning of his cheeks;
> Then with her windy sighs and golden hairs
> To fan and blow them dry again she seeks:
> He saith she is immodest, blames her 'miss;
> What follows more she murders … with a kiss.

[*Breaking the spell*] I love that poem, but I love these more.

She devours an éclair, untidily, with no hint of self-consciousness. CYRANO *is a sandpit she has played in all her life, blood-brother-and-sister.*

How are you?
CYRANO: Well … I'm well. Is there more you've come to tell …?
ROXANE: So much! But first, to thank you most of all.
Your duel! That fool you checkmated last night—

That creature—has pursued me with the height
Of insolence, of impudence. That wretch.
De Guiche, his patron sent him forth to fetch
Me for himself. De Guiche, who is of late,
Executor of my father's estate,
Would force me into marriage with Valvert,
A ploy to make me his … at least to share …
CYRANO: De Guiche? Was that his elegant disguise?
Then I fought not for my nose, but for your eyes.
ROXANE: Thank you.

Silence.

CYRANO: And so … you wish to speak with me …
ROXANE: More to confess!
I … am not one to lose my tongue! Ha!
But nor am I familiar with such … enthrallment!
I need to ask you something.
CYRANO: Anything?
ROXANE: I fear this may be asking *everything*!

Silence.

Can we start again? In fact, can we go back to the start?

> *She leaps up and flies to the door, opens it ajar and re-imagines her entry—this time gracefully, skilfully—closes it stylishly, left-handed, scoops the battered parasol from the bin, opens and parades it gracefully to the table, covers the remaining mess of half-eaten éclairs—and sits.*

To Bergerac.
CYRANO: [*confused and surprised*] To Bergerac!?
ROXANE: [*finding her feet again in the memory*] I wonder—
Are you still the same? My—almost—brother;
When we would spend those summers, children together?
Playing in the cornfield, by the lake.
CYRANO: How could I forget? At Bergerac.
ROXANE: Your shoes were shields, and bushes ambushes!
You used to cut the reeds to make your swords.
CYRANO: And you would fish the pond for buried treasures,
And string the golden corn-silk for your dolls.

ROXANE: Beanstalks were enemies—
CYRANO: And green plums bombs!
ROXANE: And blackberries!
CYRANO: And mulberries. And frogs!
ROXANE: I think just about everything was a bomb, wasn't it?
CYRANO: Just about everything, yes.

Laughter. Beat.

ROXANE: And then my wish was always your command.
CYRANO: Roxane, in her short skirts, was Madeleine ...
ROXANE: Was I fair then?
CYRANO: You were never exactly plain.

He removes the letter from his pocket.

ROXANE: I hated having to play the little sister.
So when you'd climb a tree and cut your hand,
And come running to me like a wounded bull,
I'd become your mother, gruff and rough,
And say, 'What on earth have you done now?'

Taking his hand, she tosses the letter on the table.

What on earth have you done now?

He draws back his hand.

No, let me see! [*Severe, as it used to be*] Let me see it!
At your age! Did you ever grow up?
How did this happen?
CYRANO: Oh ... playing with the big boys—by the Porte de Nesle.
ROXANE: [*dipping her handkerchief in a glass of water*] Give it here!
CYRANO: Yes, Mother!
ROXANE: Playing! And how many big boys in this game?
CYRANO: Oh! About ... a hundred.
ROXANE: Of course, about a hundred.

He doesn't appear to be joking.

About a hundred? Right, out with it, tell me!
CYRANO: No, leave it. You—you, out with it.
The thing you've come—the confession—if you dare!
ROXANE: [*keeping his hand and meeting his challenge*] I'm stronger now
for breathing that country air.

Memories of our old wars embolden me!
[*Very frank and tender*] It's like you and I are home again.
Listen.
Right.
I am in love.
CYRANO: Ah! …
ROXANE: With someone who doesn't know, doesn't suspect.
CYRANO: Ah! …
ROXANE: Not yet.
CYRANO: Ah! …
ROXANE: But he will soon.
CYRANO: Ah! …
ROXANE: He loves me too. I think. But from afar.
CYRANO: Ah.
ROXANE: From a very far, too scared to speak.
CYRANO: Ah! …
ROXANE: Can you say anything but 'Ah'?

She squeezes his hand.

CYRANO: *Aarrgh!*
ROXANE: Leave your hand; why is it so hot? D'you have a fever?
CYRANO: Aha.
ROXANE: [*back on track*] But I have seen love trembling on his lips.
CYRANO: Ah! …
DUENNA: [*crashing in*] I've eaten them all.
CYRANO: [*crashing her out*] Go read the bags.
ROXANE: [*bandaging his hand with her handkerchief*] He's a soldier, and more than that, he's in your regiment.
CYRANO: Ah! …
ROXANE: In fact, in your own company!
CYRANO: Ah! …
ROXANE: His silence hides a genius, I can tell.
He is proud and brave and strong … and beautiful.
CYRANO: [*pale*] Beautiful.
ROXANE: What's the matter?
CYRANO: Nothing—the fever—beautiful?
ROXANE: Well, handsome. Anyway … I love him, I adore him.
But I've only ever seen him at the theatre.

ACT TWO

CYRANO: Never met? Never spoken?
ROXANE: With our eyes. With our backs! Our minds!
CYRANO: How do you know then …?
ROXANE: A woman knows when she is loved.
CYRANO: Ah. He's a cadet?
ROXANE: Of the Guards.
CYRANO: His name?
ROXANE: Baron Christian de Neuvillette.
CYRANO: He is not of the Guards!
ROXANE: He joins this morning. Under your captain, Carbon de Castel-Jaloux.
CYRANO: Well—what if he's a fool—a savage?—My sweet—little 'sister'—
You need a match in thought, in words, in elegance,
What if he's a …? What if he lacks eloquence?
ROXANE: He won't! Look at his hair!
CYRANO: Ah, I see. You *are* in love.
ROXANE: I guess—I know—I feel his genius.
CYRANO: All is fair beneath a fair moustache.
ROXANE: What?
CYRANO: Nothing. Beauty needs no explanation.

Silence. CYRANO *returns the letter to his pocket.*

And so, you brought me here to tell me this?
ROXANE: No—well yes, and to ask a benefice.
Your company all come from Gascony.
Christian is from the north …
CYRANO: Ah, now I see.
You fear the rituals of Gascon pride,
That baptise those who venture from outside.
ROXANE: I've seen what they can do, the scars and scores
They settle, I'm afraid—
CYRANO: [*through gritted teeth*] Not without cause!
ROXANE: But when, last night, I saw you—when you dared—
Defy that brute—those brutes—I was so scared,
But you were breathtaking, invincible.
If thought, if only …
CYRANO: … I'd protect your fool—friend.

This Christian won't go to the lions, I promise.
ROXANE: [*using her pinkie finger*] Swear it, by our long-forgotten summers!
CYRANO: I do. I swear.
ROXANE: You'll always be his friend?
CYRANO: I'll be ... at very least, I will pretend.
ROXANE: You won't need to. And he won't be forced to duel?
CYRANO: Not today.
ROXANE: No. Not ever. That's a rule.
CYRANO: I promise.

    ROXANE *fervently embraces him, kissing his cheek.*

ROXANE: [*embracing him again*] Oh, Cyrano, I love you!
[*With overwhelming relief*] Ooh—well, you see now, that wasn't so hard!
[*Back to his hand*] Now, about you, last night, tell me! Every word.
[*Suddenly*] But I have to go! God, I do love you.
And please tell him to write, and make it soon!
CYRANO: I'll tell him.
ROXANE: You are beautiful. A hundred men!
And my boy with his bulrush sword! Ah! When,
We have the time, you must tell me—the lot!
I have to go. But please, tell him to write.
CYRANO: Yes, yes.

    Eating a puff and collecting her things, ROXANE *picks up the wrapper and finishes the earlier poem gracefully as she leaves.*

ROXANE: Now weary of the world, thus Venus hies,
    And yokes her silver doves; by whose swift aid
    Their mistress mounted through the empty skies,
    In her light chariot quickly is convey'd;
    Holding their course to Paphos, where their queen
    Means to immure herself and not be seen.

    Now at the door, a last comment:

And all alone! Such courage. A hundred men!
Au revoir.
CYRANO: I've been braver still since then.

    ROXANE *goes out.* CYRANO *stands motionless, eyes on the ground.*

A silence.

The door opens. RAGUENEAU *looks in.*

RAGUENEAU: Can we come in?

CYRANO: [*without stirring*] Yes …

RAGUENEAU *signs to his friends and they come in.*

At the same time, CARBON *enters through a door at the back, wearing captain's uniform.*

CARBON: Here he is! Cyrano.

CYRANO: [*saluting*] Captain! …

CARBON: We heard it all!

CYRANO: What!

CARBON: The Port de Nesle. The story, in prose, but we want it from you, in verse!

CYRANO: There's nothing to tell.

CARBON: And there's nothing to drink. Come on. Across the road. The cadets are the tavern.

CYRANO: No thank you.

CARBON: Then I'll bring them over.

CYRANO: No!

CARBON: Cyrano.

CYRANO: There's nothing to tell.

CARBON: A hundred to one. Cyrano.

A tale of exploits … With Europe on the brink … these boys could use a hero!

He goes to the door and calls across the street in a voice of thunder.

Over here, lads! Come on, men *can* live on bread alone!

CADETS: [*offstage*] Ah! Sandious!

Tumult outside. Noise of boots and swords is heard approaching.

CARBON: Here they come.

The CADETS *enter.*

CADETS: *Mille dious! Capdedious! Pocapdedious! Mordious!*

RAGUENEAU: Gentlemen, you are Gascons? All of you? Welcome!

FIRST CADET: [*to* CYRANO] Bravo!

CYRANO: Baron!

SECOND CADET: [*shaking his hands*] *Vivat!*
CYRANO: Baron!
THIRD CADET: Let me kiss you!
CYRANO: Baron! Bravo.
SEVERAL CADETS: [*a chant and lift*] Cyrano-Savinien-Hercule—*de Bergerac!*

    A CADET *has raised a valuable urn.*

LISE: Put that down.

    Now they are lifting anything they can see.

Put me down!
RAGUENEAU: My shop is under siege! They'll smash everything! *Magnificent!*
LE BRET: My friend, Paris is at the doorstep.
CYRANO: [*sarcastically*] Him too? Please, show him in.
LE BRET They're looking for you! A delirious mob.
CYRANO: [*alarmed*] I trust you didn't tell them where to find me!
LE BRET: I did. Tell me you have no friends!

    CYRANO *walks away.*

[*In a low voice, following*] And Roxane?
CYRANO: Quiet.

    A famous PLAYWRIGHT *parts the crowd.*

PLAYWRIGHT: *My friend!*
CYRANO: I never knew you were!
PLAYWRIGHT: Let me present you to my employers.
CYRANO: [*coldly*] And who will first present me, sir, to you?
PLAYWRIGHT: The Comédie-Française has sent me to you.
    I imagine you have rhymed five acts or so?
LE BRET: [*overjoyed*] Good God, Cyrano!
CYRANO: Perhaps.
LE BRET: [*in* CYRANO'*s ear*] Your play! Your *Agrippine*! On stage, at last.
PLAYWRIGHT: A simple meet—we have a conversation.
    We get to hear your passages at play,
    We do some rewrites, make an alteration …
    A premiere for you! And we can pay!

ACT TWO

CYRANO: Alteration?
PLAYWRIGHT: We fix a line or two.
CYRANO: Impossible! My blood congeals to think
Another hand should—fix—you say? *Mon dieu!*
Fix this!

A cream cake to the PLAYWRIGHT*'s face.*

I wouldn't let you *smell* my ink!

The PLAYWRIGHT *makes to leave.*

LE BRET: [*astonished*] What's wrong with you? That was Jean-Paul Sartre.
CYRANO: Who cares?

The PLAYWRIGHT, *confused, temporarily blinded, is doubling back.*

RAGUENEAU: Ah, that's 'No Exit'. Through here, sir.

He shepherds the PLAYWRIGHT *out.*

A movement in the crowd as DE GUICHE *appears, escorted by officers.*

FOURTH CADET: Here is Commander de Guiche?

A murmur—they come to attention.

He comes from the Marshal de Gassion …
DE GUICHE: … who would express his admiration, sir,
For your new exploit noised so loud abroad.
CROWD: Bravo!
CYRANO: [*saluting*] The marshal is the very judge of valour.

CYRANO *makes to leave.* LE BRET *grabs him.*

LE BRET: What happened? What did she say?
CYRANO: Who …?
LE BRET: I can see you're in pain.
CYRANO: Me? In front of these? You'll see!
DE GUICHE: In feats of arms, you seem to know no limits.

Another roar.

And these would be your consort.
CYRANO: My cadets!
CADETS: [*in a terrible voice*] *Of Gascony!*

CARBON: Cyrano!
CYRANO: Captain!
CARBON: Present them to my lord—
CYRANO: Yes, sir.
[*Making steps toward* DE GUICHE] My Lord de Guiche, permit that I present —

A drum, makeshift on a pastry tray, commences.

ALL CADETS: We are the Gascony Cadets,
    Of Captain de Castel-Jaloux!
    Braggers of brags 'n layers of bets
    We are the Gascony Cadets.
    We'll fight, we'll die, on land and sea,
    For Paris, France and St Denis!
    We'll fight for the roots of our family tree
    We are the boys from Gascony.

    With hearts of steel, and blood of zinc,
    We drink our fill and sink the pink,
    And even when rutting like roosters we think
    Of our Captain—de Castel-Jaloux!
    Freedom fighters—and women sighters
    We spread liberty—

CADET: I spread hepatitis!
CYRANO: We are the wolves of Gascon
    That's our Captain—our Carbon!

    Friends to none but the blade and the gun,
    Loyal to love and the Revolution,
    Addicted to blood and the heat of the sun,
    We even beat off to the beat of the drum,
    We make illegitimate babies for fun—

The next line is sung by a single CADET. *All remove their caps at the mention of 'mothers'.*

CADET: [*delicate, lyrical, high and tender*] But our mothers are pure and proud of their sons,
ALL CADETS: We're sweeter than lilies and Louis Vuitton
    The lost boys of Gascon …

Pity the enemy line that gets
In the way of us settling ancient debts,
We'll storm across his parapets,
We are the Gascony Cadets!

An awkwardly long pause—stillness for DE GUICHE *to respond to them finishing—then:*

Of Captain de Castel-Jaloux!

They conclude with a mix of respectful and belligerent intent toward DE GUICHE, *led with some fierceness by* CYRANO.

RAGUENEAU *brings an armchair for* DE GUICHE, *who seats himself with a haughty carelessness.*

DE GUICHE: You are proud, aren't you?
CYRANO: Really? You noticed that?
DE GUICHE: [*getting up to leave, in control but resisting an urge*] Don Quixote? Ever read it?
CYRANO: I could recite it.
And I doff my hat to that madman's soul!
DE GUICHE: Have a look again. The windmill chapter!
CYRANO: Chapter eight.
DE GUICHE: 'When one tilts 'gainst windmills—they may please—'
CYRANO: 'I tilt 'gainst those who change with every breeze.'
DE GUICHE: Those 'windmills'—they may please to lift their spars
And toss you in the dirt …
CYRANO: Or to the stars!

DE GUICHE *exits.* LE BRET *ushers the* CADETS *towards the back room. They exit with* RAGUENEAU, LE BRET *remains.*

LE BRET: Gentlemen … gentlemen …

He comes back to CYRANO.

[*Despairingly*] Idiot!
CYRANO: Le Bret.
LE BRET: Will you not agree that you wilfully
Seek to annihilate each chance of Fate
That might bring you success; you cannot see
That you are the enemy—
CYRANO: You exaggerate.

Beat. CYRANO *considers whether to take this matter up with his friend, knowing that once he starts, he won't stop. He starts.*

Success? There is another book worth reading.
Victor-Marie Hugo, *Les Misérables.*
Page four hundred and sixteen—he talks about 'succeeding'.
LE BRET: I don't go in for soppy melodrama.
CYRANO: It's worth a look, would you like to me to quote it?
LE BRET: I know you're going to—I may not note it.

CYRANO *perhaps removes a beloved and battered notebook from his pocket, fingering the pages to throw it before* LE BRET.

CYRANO: 'Success is an ugly thing. Men are deceived by its false resemblance to merit. They confound the brilliance of the firmament with the star-shaped footprints of a duck in the mud.'
LE BRET: Ah! Sounds good—but I might wait for the play.
CYRANO: Have a cake, Le Bret—care for an éclair?
LE BRET: I care for you, De Berg. Lay aside your pride
Long enough to bend one of those scruples.
CYRANO: Ah, compromise—
LE BRET: [*moving to exit*] Yeah—see if it kills you.
CYRANO: [*unable to contain his rage any longer*] And what then?
Once I've put one kink into those scruples
The wrinkles double, don't they? Then quadruple.
Then suddenly I'm sucking like an ivy
On some rich patron's trunk, then I'm conniving
To scale ever higher, corrupt and coarse,
Instead of growing strong by right and force.
What would you have me do? Crawl my way up?
No, thank you. Be a sycophant, and sup
With every leeching fop? Dress for success?
Write poems to my 'sponsors' like all the rest?
No, thank you. Or shall I, like the others,
Let fear and censorship and caution smother
Whatever might offend my lord and master?
No, thank you. I could whore myself much faster,
Writing three-word slogans advertising
Products—soulless campaigns subsidising

The great collective death of human passion—
Just till integrity is 'back in fashion'!
Shall I slake my morning thirst on leftovers
At the tables of aristocratic *poseurs*,
Wriggling and grovelling for advancement?
No, thanks. Or perhaps I'll learn *this* dance meant

> *Demonstrating a wild begging on his knees, he crawls toward* LE BRET.

For the pavement, till my kneecaps fester?
I'd sooner cross the street and be a jester
In that rabid circus we call Government!
Or chase me down the Catholic covenant,
And turn my hand to hymns of blind oppression,
Till I lose my sceptic's talent in confession.
No, thank you. Dining out to get ahead?
Feasting the influential? Breaking bread
With critics? Should I serve up what they want?
A disciple to the latest fucking cant?
No, thank you. No, thank you. Jump through a hoop,
To be the *big* man in a *tiny* group?
Labour to write a line of such good breeding,
Its only fault is that it's not worth reading!
No, thanks. Should I be happy just to look
For a lifetime's reputation from one book?
Acclaim? Awards and prizes? They seem petty,
When flung about in handfuls like confetti!
No—maybe I should. I'm sure my lips can pucker—

> *He manically puckers his lips high in the air.*

There! Ready to smooch! I'll 'tongue for my tucker'!
I'll cultivate the gift for condescension,
Seeking always for affection and attention
From the salons and the suck-ups—imbeciles—
Who pollute our foyers with their vapid smiles,
And kiss that flatulent arse— 'society',
Ignore the stench and cry ... *'O enchanté'.*
Everyone wants *'in'*, don't they? A key!
Well, mine's like magic ...

He draws his sword.

Open says-a-me ...

Stabbing through a bag of flour, he leaves his sword quivering in the air.

But no thanks. I'll stay *out*side, in the air,
Alone, where I can breathe. See, I can't bear
To bend over backwards till I snap my spine,
And scratch so many backs I can't find mine!
No, no, no! Thank you, no! No, thank you!
But to go ...
Free—free to dream and laugh and tilt my wing
To any song my heart tells me to sing.
To cock a leg whenever I see reason
And shoot at fools whenever they're in season.
To write without a *thought* for fame or fortune,
Recognition or a greater portion
Of respect than I can solely merit,
Alone! It's not a prize I can inherit!
I never wrote a line that didn't start
Its passage in my soul and in my heart.
Alone! A single leaf in my own garden,
My own patch, my own block I beg your pardon!
In short: I'm not a parasite. I'll be ...
... alone ... I'll be alone ... but I'll be free.

LE BRET: Alone, yes ... you will be, but not indifferent.
A man who wants true solitude's not insistent
On gathering enemies at every turn.
You sure you're not just too frightened to learn
That living means actually ... taking part?
That life's not as accommodating as art.
It's harder, blunter, duller, disappointing,
You do your best and still it leaves you wanting.
Alone? Then try the moon ... For what's it's worth,
You'll find too many friends down here on earth.

CYRANO: [*cruelly*] Like you? Like you ... with friends at every pier,
'Acquaintances', 'associates', 'connections',
But not one free, original idea

Between you all? Your minds are a confection
Of practicalities, of statements born of 'fact',
Of dullnesses and docile observation,
Nothing to elevate you from the pack.

Turning on the whole group of excited CADETS *as well:*

You crave friendship 'cause you lack imagination.
You're like one of those soft Italian collars,
Le Bret, comfortable and so ready-to-wear;
But never starched enough to help your shoulders
Hold your head from bowing here and everywhere.
My collar's stiff with hate—I love that word!
And my enemies remind me that I'm free,
They keep my head held high above the crowd.
Your friends are bondage—

LE BRET: This is lunacy!

After a silence, he takes CYRANO'*s arm.*

Well, shout your pride to anyone you want to,
But just whisper to me … she doesn't love you …
… does she?

CYRANO *has no response.*

CHRISTIAN *enters, mingled with the* CADETS, *who do not speak to him.* CYRANO *has seated himself at a table, where* LISE *serves him.*

FOURTH CADET: Come on, de Bergerac, the story.

CYRANO *turns around to a growing chant from the* CADETS.

CADETS: The story! Cyrano! Cyrano!

CYRANO *moves off to the kitchen to get a coffee, etc.*

CYRANO: In its time! *Café?* Ragueneau?

The CADETS *set up the room for* CYRANO'*s story.*

THIRD CADET: A tale of Gascon courage should be a good example for our new apprentice—

CHRISTIAN: Apprentice?

SECOND CADET: The intern will get you a coffee, Cyrano!

CHRISTIAN *doesn't bite.*

FIRST CADET: Or a soft-boiled egg. Like they eat in Normandy.
No response.
Hum! Not a man of many words!
Perhaps he stammers. Here, repeat after me:
[*Sitting in front of him*] 'What's v-v-vain, yet plain, comes mainly from T—Touraine?'

> CHRISTIAN *springs upon his throat and they hold each other in a suspended threat, joined by others.* CHRISTIAN *has a fearlessness we had not anticipated.*

CHRISTIAN: I'd watch your southern mouth if I were you.
THIRD CADET: Oooh-hoo—close call, my friend! We tend not to mention facial features around here.
CHRISTIAN: Yeah? And why's that?

A threatening intensity still pervades the room.

THIRD CADET: We show some *sense*-itivity when referencing the *'senses'*. It tends to raise an *eyebrow* round here when people have the *cheek* to give any *lip* in that particular department. So a word in your *ear*:

> *He whispers something and points in* CYRANO'*s direction—the moment genuinely appears to take* CHRISTIAN'*s interest as he listens.*

Just keep an *eye* on that, yeah?
Take out your handkerchief? It might become your shroud.

> *In the intense stillness and silence of this moment, they trick and physically humiliate* CHRISTIAN. *He rises and goes to* CARBON, *who has feigned to see nothing.*

CHRISTIAN: [*at attention*] Captain!
CARBON: Private!
CHRISTIAN: A word of advice, sir?
CARBON: I wasn't aware I needed your advice, young man.
CHRISTIAN: [*again, no conversation is ever easy for* CHRISTIAN] No, pardon, sir ... I mean I would request your advice ... to me ... from you ... sir!

Silence.

Go?

ACT TWO

CARBON: Go!
CHRISTIAN: Thank you, sir.
What do you give to southerners sick with their own pride?
CARBON: A promotion usually.

> CHRISTIAN *doesn't appreciate, or perhaps get, the joke*—CARBON, *instead, gets to the point.*

You want these boys to respect you, lad?
CHRISTIAN: [*surprised by the frankness of the question*] … I suppose— yes, sir.
CARBON: On your first morning? Well … you could try a miracle.

> *A good leader, he opens a subtle door of inspiration.*

Give 'em a bit of good northern medicine, if you think you can apply the dose.
CHRISTIAN: Thank you, sir!

> CHRISTIAN *moves to dress in his new uniform as* CYRANO *re-enters.*

CADETS: [*to* CYRANO] Now the story! The Port de Nesle! Cyrano versus the French Legion!
CYRANO: [*coming toward them*] The story? …

> *All bring their stools up and group around him, listening eagerly.* CHRISTIAN *is changing into his clean, new, Gascon uniform— yes, a contrivance to have him shirtless and looking spectacular by the time* CYRANO *clears the room and meets his rival—Adonis.*

Well, I was alone, despite my forty followers!
The moon, a silver clock, hung in the sky,
Pensive, counting down to pandemonium.
When suddenly …

> *Deliberately building their expectation, then disappointing, his mood improves simply through having an audience.*

… clouds, cloud cover, couldn't see a thing,

> *The* CADETS, *hanging on his every breath, explode at him in ribald humour.*

God had closed his clock-case for the night.
Blackness. Liquid darkness. Thick as ink.

Thick as the drink we love in Gascony!

Almost painful gyrations from his boys at the memory.

Thick as that night in Spain in '93.

A new ripple of sober remembrance from the older soldiers.

The Seine was just a murmur now, a rumour ...
You couldn't see your hand in front of your—
CHRISTIAN: Nose?

Silence. All slowly rise, looking in terror at CYRANO, *who has stopped—dumbfounded. Pause.*

CYRANO: Who on God's earth is that?
FIRST CADET: [*stunned*] A new cadet, he joined this morning.
CYRANO: [*already moving toward* CHRISTIAN] This morning?
CARBON: Yes ... his name is ... [*consulting* CHRISTIAN'*s papers*] Baron Christian de Neuvil ...
CYRANO: [*checking himself suddenly*] Good! That's excellent. Good. Good.

He turns pale, flushes, makes as if to crush CHRISTIAN.

I ...
[*Controlling himself*] Where was I?
[*With a burst of rage*] Mordious! ...
[*Continuing calmly*] Your hand ... in front of your face. Darkness.

Astonishment. The CADETS *reseat themselves, staring at him.*

I edged my way through fog out to the Quay,
A thirty-foot drop to the riverbank,
One mis-step, I break my—
CHRISTIAN: Nose?

Everyone starts up. CHRISTIAN *reaches for his sword.*

CYRANO: [*in a choked voice*] My neck!
I'd break my neck! I was starting to regret sticking—
CHRISTIAN: Your nose?
CYRANO: My neck ... out for a friend! A drunkard!
I realise I could end up paying—
CHRISTIAN: Through the nose—
CYRANO: Dearly for this.

ACT TWO

But I thought, 'On, Gascon! A duty to protect!'
I venture to the narrowest point of the pier.
To contain their attack. I know Spartan warfare
Like the back of my—
CHRISTIAN: Nose.
CYRANO: Hand. Hand! A first glint of steel
Flashes from the dark. I parry and find myself ...
CHRISTIAN: Nose to nose ...
CYRANO: [*springing from his seat, barely controlling himself*] Face to face ...

The CADETS *baulk in their seats.*

... with countless brawling toughs,
I charge, run through two, a third I take the midriff,
Not killed, but he'll need—
CHRISTIAN: Rhinoplasty!
CYRANO: [*struggling*] Surgery, he'll need an operation ... on his ... stomach.
I spin, I flay—
CHRISTIAN: My nostrils,
CYRANO: My *blade*, and cut a fourth, fifth, sixth,
Where they'll come from next, heaven—
CHRISTIAN: Nose.
CYRANO: Knows. Yes, nose, [*head in hands, almost baffled*] heaven knows, yes, good.
I gore another, impale him, take the eighth
A brutal blow on the ...

He holds to allow an interruption, trying to disarm CHRISTIAN. *No response.*

... head. He screams, I laugh,
These cries are—
CHRISTIAN: Mucus to my ears.
CYRANO: *Music* ... to me. A symphony of pain.
Another takes aim, I drive him to the bridge—
CHRISTIAN: Of my nose—
CYRANO: A mistake perhaps, I'm flanked. I fear I've put the—
CHRISTIAN: Cartilage before the horse?

CYRANO: *Cart. Cart.* It's the cart I've put before the—
CHRISTIAN: Snot?
CYRANO: Horse. I'm surrounded. Quiet falls. I'm in the eye of the—
CHRISTIAN: Snort.
CYRANO: Storm. [*Delirious now*] I'm in the storm of the snot. Snort of the storm. You ... you—
CHRISTIAN: Nose what I mean.
CYRANO: Understand me, yes?

> *The* CADETS, *in shock, nod in unison.*

They descend upon me, eighty, ninety men.
For the first time in my life, I—
CHRISTIAN: Sneeze.
CYRANO: I freeze! I think of mortality. Then think of Gascony.

> *A roar from his fellows—the room now in a frenzy.*

And chaos is come again.

> *Another roar.*

They attack—
Thrust, parry, guard, *mezzo, misura, punta,* pif, paf—

> CHRISTIAN *throws a huge 'sneeze' into the soundscape and that's it.*
>
> CYRANO *is calm, the white calm of sincere fury.*

Get out! All of you! Off you go! Thank you. Cheers.

> *The* CADETS *rush to the doors.*

RAGUENEAU: [*handing to* CHRISTIAN, *solemn*] All I can offer you is a napkin. I'm sorry.

> *All exit except* CYRANO *and* CHRISTIAN, *who are face to face, looking at each other for a moment.* CYRANO *drives toward him, unsheathing his sword,* CHRISTIAN *whips his out.* CYRANO *drops the blade on a table very unexpectedly and opens his arms.*

CYRANO: Give me a hug.
CHRISTIAN: Sir ...
CYRANO: Embrace me.
CHRISTIAN: What?
CYRANO: You're a brave man.

CHRISTIAN: But …
CYRANO: No, I like your pluck.
CHRISTIAN: What?
CYRANO: Very much. I expected you to crack.
  Come on. I am her brother, don't forget.
CHRISTIAN: Whose?
CYRANO: Hers! Roxane's!
CHRISTIAN: Oh, God, you're not …
CYRANO: Well, 'friend' … 'brother', it's a nickname really.
CHRISTIAN: Did she say …?
CYRANO: She said.
CHRISTIAN: What did she say?
CYRANO: What you think she said.
CHRISTIAN: That … she loves me?
CYRANO: Loves, likes, passing interest perhaps.
CHRISTIAN: [*taking his hand*] I am so glad to meet you. [*Remembering himself*] Sir!
CYRANO: I think that's what we call a change of heart.
CHRISTIAN: Forgive me, I'm sorry, please forgive me.

  CHRISTIAN *is standing before him—honest, simple, shirt in hand, effortlessly attractive.*

CYRANO: It's true though, isn't it? You are a handsome bast—devil.
CHRISTIAN: Oh, sir, if you knew how much I admire you …
CYRANO: Particularly my nose by the sound of it.
CHRISTIAN: [*retrospectively awed*] I take that back, every word, every sniff. Sorry!
CYRANO: Roxane expects a letter.
CHRISTIAN: Oh … don't say that, please no.
CYRANO: What?
CHRISTIAN: I'm lost if I open my *mouth*! To *write* … I can't.
CYRANO: Why not?
CHRISTIAN: [*deeply flummoxed*] I, I … It's … I'm a fool. I'll die of shame!
CYRANO: You were confident enough in that nasal skirmish.
CHRISTIAN: Oh, that's nothing, that's a battle cry.
  I can manage mess-hall banter, but love …
  Love is nothing like war.
CYRANO: Ever read a Russian novel?

CHRISTIAN: I mean I could never … tell a woman how I love her.
CYRANO: [*aside*] You're not the only one.
   [*Back to* CHRISTIAN] I'm all eloquence on the other hand,
   If only my face were more expertly planned.
CHRISTIAN: Ha ha! Yeah.
   Sorry. That rhymed … it … um …
   I don't know how well you know her—Roxane—
   But she's … intellectual, bookish, athletic … apparently,
   She's just … good at stuff.
CYRANO: Oh, I think I probably know her well enough.
   She's a hopeless yachtsman if that's any consolation!
CHRISTIAN: [*earnestly surprised*] She's a yachtsman?
      Silence.
   Sorry!
   God—if I could express myself with grace …
CYRANO: If I could wake up from this nightmare with that face …
CHRISTIAN: There's that rhyming thing again. Oh,
   What I could do with your wit!
CYRANO: [*abruptly*] Now there's a point, why don't you borrow it?
CHRISTIAN: What?
CYRANO: Borrow it! And in return you lend
   To me what you possess, that cunning blend
   Of youth and beauty. We'll win your Venus!
   [*Becoming excited*] There's a great romantic hero somewhere between us.
CHRISTIAN: What do you mean?
CYRANO: Let me give you the words to woo Roxane.
   My articulate spirit … and your tan.
CHRISTIAN: You're asking me to lie?
CYRANO: Well, if you like.
   But a lie is like a myth if taken right.
   And a myth is like the truth in certain light!
   All you need's a tongue. I can provide it.
CHRISTIAN: That won't work!
CYRANO: You won't know till you've tried it.
CHRISTIAN: I'd be too frightened.
CYRANO: What—you're not already?

ACT TWO

> Too scared to face the girl? Your legs unsteady,
> Your heart in palpitations, bathed in sweat,
> For a meeting you've barely dreamed of yet!
> What scares you is the thought of being alone
> With her, just her and you, under the moon,
> Under her roof, her spell ... under her covers ...
> Don't fear. I'll be beside you. Two blood brothers.

CHRISTIAN: Okay ...
> I'm not sure how things go in Gascony.
> In Touraine, three's a crowd, two's company!

CYRANO: I mean beside you in pure inspiration,
> Your antidote to fear, a collaboration
> For the ages, it's the stuff of classic drama.
> The actor—he's the hero, he's the charmer!
> And the poet—he's unseen—the puppeteer—

CHRISTIAN: I'm not a puppet—

CYRANO: No! I'm not being clear.
> I mean the poet is the ... God ... behind the curtain.

CHRISTIAN: And now you're God! Look, I'm a bit uncertain.
> This sounds like madness.

CYRANO: Listen!

CHRISTIAN: No, you listen, to me!
> If she found out—

CYRANO: She won't—

CHRISTIAN: She might—

CYRANO: *Let's see!*

CHRISTIAN: Your eyes are shining! What's in this for you?

> *Beat—danger.*

CYRANO: Good question ... good ... my motives? Well ... in few,
> I am ... an artist, and my art ... is dead,
> While it remains in abstract ... in my head.
> I can sculpt, but without stone, what is the use?
> While my words stall in my mind, they're an excuse
> To hide, to shelter from the world's redress,
> From what I fear the most ...

CHRISTIAN: What's that?

CYRANO: Success.

Look, it's simple. To me, it's an amusement.
CHRISTIAN: And I am very grateful for your enthusement—

Beat.

CYRANO: —iasm, but good. Then come. Let's make a whole
From our two better halves—your lips, my soul.

A final decision rests with CHRISTIAN.

CHRISTIAN: Let's do it! Ha! What first?
CYRANO: You need a letter!
CHRISTIAN: [*a return of immediate despair*] Oh, Christ!
CYRANO: There.
CHRISTIAN: What's that?
CYRANO: I can do better,
But this is a good prelude to the best,
An idyll, in fourths, just needs an address.
CHRISTIAN: I don't quite …
CYRANO: … understand … where this has come from?
It's practice … an epithalamium!
An exercise in romantic, euphonic wit,
Just flexing muscles, all poets do it.
Wouldn't be caught dead without a verse
In our top pocket, something to rehearse,
A lyric styling, an airy nothing—Here …

Handing it, hesitant to release it:

… the more eloquent for being so insincere.
CHRISTIAN: But won't it be too … general for my love?
Are you sure it will fit Roxane?
CYRANO: Like a glove.

Silence. Something has been struck between them—selfish and selfless all at once.

CHRISTIAN: Thank you.

They embrace. The CADETS, RAGUENEAU *and the* MUSKETEER *appear in the doorway.*

THIRD CADET: What in Jesus' name!
FOURTH CADET: My Holy Mother …

ACT TWO

RAGUENEAU: Attack one nostril and he turns the other!
MUSKETEER: So at last, we can talk about his nose!
Watch this, my Lise!—Who smells something gross?

> *Pulling out several stops at once, the* MUSKETEER *kisses* LISE *passionately. He then throws flour at the door and draws a human profile in it with his finger, replete with giant nose, before returning to his theme.*

Little Ragueneau's oven's burning, get on the wire!
[To CYRANO] Do you smell smoke?

> CYRANO *draws a vast nasal breath.*

CYRANO: Where there's smoke there's fire.

> *He punches him ferociously through the doors and into the street.*

END OF ACT TWO

ACT THREE

ROXANE'S KISS

A small square in the old Marais. Old houses. Roxane's house and the wall of her garden overhung with thick foliage. Window and balcony over the door. A bench in front. From the bench and the stones jutting out of the wall, it is easy to climb to the balcony.

As the curtain rises, the DUENNA *is seated on the bench.* RAGUENEAU *is with her.*

The window on Roxane's balcony is wide open.

DUENNA: Why do you always wear black?

RAGUENEAU: I'm in mourning for my wife.
   She left me—ran off—absconded with a captain in the Tenth Champagne Regiment. She loved men in uniform.
   Beat.
   She loved men out of uniform.

DUENNA: And the shop?

RAGUENEAU: Closed.

DUENNA: All those pastries?

RAGUENEAU: Disposed.

DUENNA: Oh my! So … you're alone?

RAGUENEAU: [*angling for her interest*] Alone, solitary, unaccompanied … singular.

DUENNA: Those poor pastries! Where are they now?

RAGUENEAU: Thrown away. Dumped.

DUENNA: [*the loss is incomprehensible*] Oh my … like a mass grave … you must have despaired.

RAGUENEAU: Well yes, I locked the doors and put my head in the casserole oven but La Société Thermique shut the power off … I hadn't paid the bills. I threw myself in the Seine but I think it was the shallow end. I drank some water, I thought the sewerage might kill me, but Cyrano came along and dragged me out. He brought me here and begged Mademoiselle Madeleine to take me as her steward.

ACT THREE

DUENNA: [*sharply*] Which means you work for me!
RAGUENEAU: Yes, madame.
DUENNA: What do you know of stewardship?
RAGUENEAU: Ah ... well, I know ... absolutely nothing.
DUENNA: [*taking a set of keys from her neck and selecting one*] The flour is in the central larder with the eggs and milk, the pecans and fruit beneath the dough board—off you go and don't return without at least a quiche. [*Yelling lovingly*] Roxane, we just hired a cook!
RAGUENEAU: Thank you, madame. [*Asking her in*] May I ... cook for two?
DUENNA: Oh, I—ah—you may—but we are expected at the cinema. *The Tender Passion.*
RAGUENEAU: *The Tender Passion!* Ah, that one!
DUENNA: Yes ... the ... tender one ... have you seen it?
RAGUENEAU: I've been it!
DUENNA: Ah ... *Roxane!* We're late ... *We'll miss the discourse on the ...* um ...
RAGUENEAU: *Tender Passion.*
ROXANE: [*voice*] I'm coming. Don't get your knickers in a knot.

Embarrassed laughter from the newly courting pair.

DUENNA: [*just confirming*] They're not. In a knot.

A sound of stringed instruments approaching.

*S*urprised, *the* DUENNA *catches the departing* RAGUENEAU— *perhaps they briefly dance.*

Oh, we're being serenaded!

CYRANO *enters, flanked by* LIGNIERE *and another* MUSICIAN—*a page, pursuing him with music.*

CYRANO: That is the flattest B flat I've ever heard.
ROXANE: [*calling within*] Is that Cyrano?
CYRANO: [*in his most exuberantly playful mood thus far in the story*] It is.

Smelling a collection of flowers on her wall:

Just whiffing your sweet nectar from the street!
Your irises and gerberas and lilies;

Perhaps if I can swear to wipe my feet
I can come inside and sniff your fleur-de-lys!
DUENNA: Monsieur de Bergerac!
RAGUENEAU: Cyrano!

ROXANE *appears on the balcony—unperturbed, as if this smutty playfulness has become part of their relationship in recent times—two minds that resist typical customs of behaviour, highly individual.*

ROXANE: Oh, ignore him. His entendres and sordid euphemisms only further demonstrate the difference between man and man.
CYRANO: Oh? ... Between which man and which man? No, let me guess ... between Christian and the rest of Europe.
ROXANE: No, between Christian and the male species. I'm coming down.
DUENNA: [*pointing to the* MUSICIANS] And who are these two stringed instruments of torture?
CYRANO: Oh, I saved his life and this is my prize slash punishment—a full month's musical haunting. I know how Wagner's wife felt. Listen. [*Writing an address for the musos*] Head to the Boulevard Montmartre, number 304. It's Montfleury's house. There is a third-floor window, the fat clown's bathroom. He should be beaching himself in there around now. Play a recurring fugue until you see either the dawn or blubber oozing through the stones.
[*To the* DUENNA] So, madame, is he being a gentlemen, this poet-Adonis, Christian de—de Nervy ... Nervous-idiot—
DUENNA: Christian de Neuvillette.
ROXANE: [*coming out of the house and gripping the doorway in delight*] Even his name is handsome!
CYRANO: And yesterday's correspondence? Does he scale new heights or at last show signs of vertigo?
ROXANE: He is a pilot in uncharted space.
CYRANO: Oh, heavens, we should send a search.
ROXANE: It would need to reach heaven, his mind's flight begins at the moon and mounts ever upward.
CYRANO: The moon? My favourite motif, but a pale and chaste subject for a lover!
ROXANE: Not in his pen, it's glow is ever more brilliant. Even *you* pale in comparison with his wit, Cyrano.

CYRANO: I stand defeated. Witty then and not pale ... but ... is he chaste?
DUENNA: Monsieur, you pry! A lady never—
ROXANE: [*enjoying these nightly rituals of attention*] No, forgive him his thirst for gossip, aunt, he's a sucker for scandal. I think he's given up poetry and writes for the *Gazette*! Well—today's report—Christian remains a perfect gentlemen, he's barely stolen the impression of my hand ... I wish he would.
CYRANO: Writer's fatigue perhaps.
ROXANE: Then I forgive him. [*Suddenly very frank*] I have never in my life known anyone able to express the unknowable, the impossible minutiae of love. He says nothings that are yet ... everything. And it's not just a 'telling' of love, a tired confession, it's a dissertation, an analysis, he disassembles the very machinery of love—it's almost unromantic. He can leave love in pieces on the floor, each one distinctly separate and meaningless without its fellow, and suddenly, with no semblance of effort, he rebuilds it with a phrase—complete, refreshed, and overwhelming. His inspiration fails sometimes, it's odd, he seems to stumble and his muse collapses, but then comes another burst of grace.

Silence.

CYRANO: So not just a pretty face.
ROXANE: Oh, you men with your eternal conception that beauty and brilliance can't co-exist.
CYRANO: Oh, they can, just not on this planet. So he speaks well, how is he between sheets—of paper?
ROXANE: [*reciting*] 'The more of my poor heart you take
    The more you do restore,
    Take more again, and more I'll make,
    Take less, you'll find it more.'

    CYRANO *is in physical pain at the sound—perhaps a partly genuine cringe at the artist's own work.*

CYRANO: Oh, God—did he steal that from a child? A wind-up toy!

    RAGUENEAU, DUENNA *and* ROXANE *make simultaneous protests of the poem's quality, but* CYRANO *won't have it.*

[*Very fired up about it*] No, come on, it's a bland anaphora, a *chastush*-tic rhythm—practically medieval—a Russian folk singer just sung that to his wife and she smashed his balalaika. We just heard the invention of synthetic poetry! I'm surprised he didn't trip on that trope and break his finger!

ROXANE: [*again, by heart*]
> 'I pressed through darkness with my fingertips,
> So douse the light and read this with your lips.'

Silence.

CYRANO: Oh, that's quite good, isn't it?

Beat.

It's polysyllabic at least.

ROXANE: You're jealous.

CYRANO: [*caught out?*] What?

ROXANE: Of another poet's gifts. You needn't be, yours are very good too, just of a ... different ilk, and the war needs soldiers who can scribble.

Beat—hard to discern whether the insult was entirely accidental.

Oh, and listen to this ...

CYRANO: You know them off by heart?

DUENNA: All of them.

CYRANO: [*enchanted*] Very flattering.

ROXANE: He's a genius.

DUENNA: [*coming down quickly*] Here comes Commander de Guiche!

To CYRANO, *pushing him toward the house:*

In with you! He must not see you here, it might put him on the scent ...

CYRANO: On the scent?

ROXANE: [*to* CYRANO] Of my own dear secret! Where is Christian?
If de Guiche sees him here, he'll cruel everything.

CYRANO: He's still pursuing you?

DUENNA: In earnest. Go.

CYRANO *disappears into the house.* DE GUICHE *appears.*

ROXANE: [*curtsying to* DE GUICHE *and leaving with her aunt*] Bonsoir, we were just going out.

DE GUICHE: I came to say goodbye.

ROXANE: You're leaving?

ACT THREE

words will crash out ... and grab her ... take no prisoners ... my father taught me that.
CYRANO: Your mother must have enjoyed their dates.
CHRISTIAN: Yeah, well mock me, I'm used to being mocked, but at least I know how to take a woman in my arms.
CYRANO: Very well.

    ROXANE *and* DUENNA *return.*

Chookas.
CHRISTIAN: Take the night off.
DUENNA: Damned zeppelins, I was looking forward to that film.
ROXANE: Well, you won't see much if they start dropping munitions, like they did in March.
Christian! You came! Who needs a romantic comedy when I have a personal rhapsody to look forward to? And on such a night as this. Goodnight, good aunt. Put out the lights, [*touching her own eyelids to suggest sleep*] and then put out the lights! Understood?
DUENNA: Don't do anything *you* wouldn't do. Goodnight, young man. I hope you brought your balalaika.

    DUENNA *exits.*

CHRISTIAN: What?
ROXANE: Nothing. But ... us!
The air is sweet.
We are alone.
We have a seat.
Before the sirens come,
Shall we talk?
Shall you talk, while I listen.

    Silence.

Sorry—are you underway because I've already started—listening ...

    At length:

CHRISTIAN: I love you.
ROXANE: Good title! Now ... turn the leaf ...
CHRISTIAN: I love you.
ROXANE: Simple beginnings ... clever ... what odyssey awaits?
CHRISTIAN: I love you so much.

ROXANE: Ah, suspense, very good. Give me your worst, I can take it!
CHRISTIAN: So much. So much love.
ROXANE: That's the theme, any variations?
CHRISTIAN: You love me too. I know you do.
ROXANE: A confident protagonist, does he live till Act Two?
CHRISTIAN: I want you. Do you want me as well?
ROXANE: [*bewildered by his tone*] Hi there, have we met? I'm Madeleine, and you are …?
CHRISTIAN: Your neck is great. It's really—I want to kiss your throat.
ROXANE: Really?
CHRISTIAN: I love you.
ROXANE: Yes, that chapter's gone to print. *How* do you love me?
    Pause.
CHRISTIAN: A lot.
ROXANE: Oh, tie me down—I feel weightless! What are you doing, Christian? I'm starting to pray for bombs.
CHRISTIAN: I'm telling you I love you.
ROXANE: Yes, over and over. I said give me your worst—mission accomplished. Now surprise me.
CHRISTIAN: [*going for shock tactics*] I don't love you.
ROXANE: Oooohhhhh!
CHRISTIAN: I adore you.
ROXANE: Aaaahhhhh. The twist!
CHRISTIAN: So much!
ROXANE: *Aaannnddd*—Epilogue—Close the book—Lights out—Go to bed—Should have read the blurb—Goodnight, Christian.
CHRISTIAN: Forgive me, Roxane—I'm an idiot. I'm so in love, I'm a fool. Another chance …
ROXANE: It happens to every man, they say. Alright, take a breath. A final word …?
CHRISTIAN: It's in my heart, my love for you.
    It's in my head, it's in there too,
    It's also in lots of other things,
    Without you, it just stings … it stings.
ROXANE: [*considering it, astonished, with unspeakable anger*] I don't think that's a poem, I don't think … that can be classified as a poem. I don't recognise that as even … French. Are you speaking French?

ACT THREE

CHRISTIAN: Roxane, listen, I want to talk to you.
ROXANE: And yet ... you don't. Don't stay up too late.
CHRISTIAN: But I—
ROXANE: I know. You love me. Goodnight, Christian.

ROXANE slams the door. Silence.

CYRANO: Well, that went well.

CHRISTIAN is still in shock.

Shouldn't you do something?—prisoner's escaping.
CHRISTIAN: Shut up. Help me.
CYRANO: Oh no. It's my night off.
CHRISTIAN: Help me. I'll die.
CYRANO: You idiot, what do you expect me to do?
CHRISTIAN: Wait. A light.
CYRANO: What light?
CHRISTIAN: Through yonder window.
CYRANO: Breaks.

No recognition of the phrase from CHRISTIAN.

Oh God!
CHRISTIAN: I will die without her.
CYRANO: Shhh.

Silence.

It is very dark ...
CHRISTIAN: Please.
CYRANO: You don't deserve it ... Stand there ... under the window.
You speak, I prompt.
CHRISTIAN: But—
CYRANO: No buts. You speak. I prompt.
CHRISTIAN: Right. In what order?
CYRANO: As the word suggests, prompting comes first.
CHRISTIAN: Yep. Good. It was just you said ... ah ...
CYRANO: I think we're clear now. Call her.

The MUSICIANS re-enter suddenly, desperately out of breath.

LIGNIERE: Monsieur ... we serenaded Montfleury ... he didn't like it ... he chased us ... he's quite fit for a big man ... quite good over short distances ...

MUSICIAN: And hills, down hills ... very quick. I think we lost him though ... he dropped his towel ...
CYRANO: Good God. Then you've had quite a fright. Now, go to the corner of the street. You hear approaching feet, anyone, play something—Wait—sad tune for a man, cheerful for a woman ...
MUSICIAN: What if it's Montfleury?
CYRANO: Scream.

> *The* MUSICIANS *go.*

Call her.
CHRISTIAN: [*calling*] Roxane!
CYRANO: Try a pebble.

> CHRISTIAN *puts the pebble in his mouth and calls again.*

CHRISTIAN: Roxane!
CYRANO: Oh God ...!
ROXANE: Who's that?

> CHRISTIAN *celebrates the success of contact but is unsure how to proceed.*

CYRANO: [*whispering*] You.
CHRISTIAN: You.
 I mean me. I. Christian.
ROXANE: Oh, you!
CHRISTIAN: I need to talk to you.
CYRANO: Quietly, that's the way.
ROXANE: I'm still recovering from our last conversation.
CHRISTIAN: Please.
ROXANE: Your love expired with your intellect.
CHRISTIAN: [*prompted now*] No, my desire makes me circumspect
 When I close within the circle of your gaze.
 How can such love be captured in a phrase?
ROXANE: Better—but probably a fluke.
CHRISTIAN: Love's not a child, easily restrained,
 It won't be cradled, coddled or contained;
 A brat, its temper surges with such violence;
 I tried to speak—it wailed me to silence.
ROXANE: Better again—but mixing metaphors.

ACT THREE

CHRISTIAN: There's too much I need to say to keep the 'score',
 I've just sufficient strength to get them out,
 These words—strangled within by pride and doubt.
ROXANE: By doubt? Is that why you seem so uncertain?
 Your words are strange and slow—
CYRANO: [*unable to restrain a response, almost involuntarily*] It's just the curtain
 Of the night, its heavy folds thicken thought—
 [*To* CHRISTIAN] This is getting difficult, we'll get caught,
 You stand aside, I'll whisper—
ROXANE: What was that?
CYRANO: Nothing, just had to … clear away a rat.

> CHRISTIAN *gestures in accusation for that one.* CYRANO *gestures apology, just thinking on his feet …*

ROXANE: Oh God, well that's one way to spoil the mood.
CYRANO: No, nothing Paris sends us can intrude,
 Upon this moment—filthy streets can do no harm,
 Nor sewers, vermin—

> *The* MUSICIANS *scream in the distance, as if* MONTFLEURY *is approaching.*

LIGNIERE: [*offstage*] Sorry, false alarm!
CYRANO: These ancient streets can hold a thousand ills,
 But none can spoil how this moment fills
 My heart. My lips are desperate to relieve them
 Of these sighs; your ears are careless to believe them
 But I'll try. My words were slow with you above me,
 They had to climb through fears that you won't love me,
 Your words can fall with ease from such a height,
 But now I've found my feet—
ROXANE: Stand in the light,
 I want to see you. Stay there, I'll come down.
CYRANO/CHRISTIAN: No/No!
ROXANE: Why such a vehement no? Was that two sounds …?
CYRANO: An echo …
CHRISTIAN: … echo … echo …

> CYRANO *stands dumbfounded at* CHRISTIAN*'s assistance, then back to the task:*

CYRANO: Night and silence never lack
  That Parisian arrogance to answer back.
  But now my words have found rhythm and rhyme;
  You can't descend, when they've just learned to climb.
ROXANE: But I want to see you, stand up on the bench.
CYRANO: Let's not forgo this unexpected chance
  To dance and mingle voices in the dark.
  Let's blindfold love and see if it can spark
  Imaginings we never knew we had.
  You clothed in light, myself in darkness clad.
  It's glorious for me be to this lost,
  Just a shadow moving and you a ghost.
  It's perfect, just to speak with you—unseen—
ROXANE: Unseen?
CYRANO: Unhindered ... disembodied ... clean!
ROXANE: But I'm so far from you.
CYRANO: [*joyous*] And so you should be,
  One harsh word from there is like a wood beam
  Thrown from a building, you can strike me down;
  If I displease you—break me with a sound!
ROXANE: [*caught in it now*] I won't, I never would;
CYRANO: If you could know,
  How much this means to me, how far I'd go,
  To win you. Fool! I wish I could express it.
ROXANE: You have! Your words—
CYRANO: [*deeply judging himself*] I know—they were excessive,
  Indulgent. Until now, I've never spoken
  The truth, from my own heart, laid bare and open—
ROXANE: Why not?
CYRANO: Because I've had to speak it through ...
  Beat.
ROXANE: Through what?
CYRANO: Through ignorance, a sort of blue
  Mist of drunkenness.
ROXANE: So they were lies?
CHRISTIAN: Cyrano!?

CYRANO: No! 'Truth' ... but we can't map a paradise;
We can't express perfection; what's sublime
Is just this chance to speak for the first time.
ROXANE: The first time. Yes. Even your voice has changed.
CYRANO: That's true. It has. It must. It's rearranged
My being. To speak a language I don't know
I need new voice, new sense, a new credo,
I need this ... inky cloak ... because the night
Protects me, I can dare to claim the right
To be myself. I'm speaking ... ah ... what have I said?
I'm sorry ... forgive me ... I seem to have strayed
Into new worlds—
ROXANE: New?
CYRANO: Yes, without the fear
You'll mock me. Or you'll laugh. See, I can bear
Almost anything but—
ROXANE: Mock you ... for what?
CYRANO: For my ... stupidity; my foolish plot
To win you with such verbal decoration,
Floral bouquets of the imagination,
Letters reeking of self-conscious pride,
Linguistic bubbles—throw them all aside—
ROXANE: Your letters? No, I won't.
CYRANO: Then never read them!
ROXANE: What are you saying? Your verses ... I concede they're ...
floral ... but the sweetness of those flowers—
CYRANO: Is sickening, their perfumed fragrance sours
Meaning; they're toys—
ROXANE: [*angered by his belligerence*] They may be, but they're ours!
CYRANO: Not tonight. Not tonight. Tonight we're learning
How to walk again, tonight we're burning
Everything; these stale Valentines,
These hearts and arrows, even shallow rhymes
Have had their day. That's it! What are they worth,
Compared to the wild urge to speak the truth?

A moment comes—and God help those for whom
It never comes—when it won't matter what

We say. When love becomes a faith, we pray,
Not with clever words but with whatever
We can find to reach each other …
ROXANE: And if that moment has now come for us,
What words will you say to me?
CYRANO: All of them.
Every one I know. All words that ever were,
Or weren't, or could or couldn't be, I'll hurl
In great armfuls across the summer world,
Until they make together all one sound—
I love you. I love you. I couldn't love you more
If there were two of me, if there were four, I
Choke with love, you're the colour of my dreams,
I taste you in the air, I hear your name,
In every thing, in every sound there is,
In every silence, every thud and crash,
You're the hope in every wish I've ever had—
I'm sorry, I can't think—I never knew
These chimes could ring for me. And so for you!
You are Roxane—Rox … ane—your name is like a bell,
In bronze, in brazen gold it swings and tells
Me every little thing you ever do,
No triviality is ever lost
On me. I remember forgotten things
Like they were yesterday—the twelfth of May—
You changed the way you wore your hair, it fell
A little to the left—you didn't like it,
But I thought it worked. And do you know how
When you look a little too long at the sun,
That disk of fire floats on everything,
Everywhere you look you see more suns?
Your mind is like that solar flare to me,
I close my eyes, it's all that I can see.
ROXANE: Thank you. Yes, yes, that is love.
CYRANO: You're trembling!
I feel it in the vines, I feel your blood
Beating its silent march along these spines

Of flowers, fleeting down these slender towers
To my song. I hear you listening—to me;
To my words. It's my love that makes these leaves
Of jasmine shiver like a filament
That weaves our souls together. I could never,
In my most stupid, unreasonable dreams,
Have hoped to make you know how much it means
To say I love you.
ROXANE: Me too. I do. I am.
I don't know what I'm saying—I'm sorry—
Why am I crying?—Roxane!—You've made me,
I don't know. I love you. I love you—a lot.
CYRANO: You do? I know you do. And that's … it …!
That's all that life can be, that is the task
That death waits for, no more that I could ask.

> *Seeing his face in the reflection of her downstairs window, the eternal question comes to his mind.*

Unless it be to … it would be remiss
For me to fail to … ask you …
CHRISTIAN: For a kiss.
CYRANO: [*to* CHRISTIAN] What!?
ROXANE: What?
CYRANO: [*to* ROXANE] What?
ROXANE: Did you say something?
CYRANO: No. Did you?
ROXANE: No, did you? I thought you did.
CYRANO: I don't think I was talking …
ROXANE: But you were asking … for a … did you say—?
CYRANO: No. I didn't. Nothing. [*To* CHRISTIAN] It's too soon! Idiot!
CHRISTIAN: Why? We're there, she's ready, the state she's in …
What else next? It's time. You know the theme,
'Take no prisoners' …
ROXANE: Take no what?
CYRANO: … no business,
That is not mine and put … my nose in it …
When it's not my business … [*to* CHRISTIAN] to ask … for things …
ROXANE: You did ask. And you can ask more than that.

CYRANO: I can? I won't. It's right that you object.
ROXANE: I don't object.
CHRISTIAN: She don't object.
CYRANO: 'Doesn't'! Doesn't!
   Shut up, Christian!
ROXANE: What did you say?
CYRANO: I told myself to shudder, to 'Shudder Christian'
   At the impertinence of such a question.
   Wait, someone's coming.

   ROXANE *disappears.*

By the sound of it—a woman *and* a man,
Ah, I see—a priest.

   CAPUCHIN *enters.*

CAPUCHIN: Hello there, friends. I'm looking for—Robin.
   Madeleine Robin.
CHRISTIAN: Why? What for?
CYRANO: For good reason, I'm sure.
   At the bottom of the hill, friend. Straight on.
CAPUCHIN: The *bottom* of the hill. For *Christ's sake* ...!
   And his sake alone, I continue on …
   Farewell, my friends. Have you anything to confess?
   I will pray for you, my son. God loves all his children.
   And thank you for your courage in the days
   Ahead of us. We're all behind you boys.

   CAPUCHIN *exits.*

CYRANO: Yes, around a hundred and forty miles behind us usually.
CHRISTIAN: Now, get that kiss for me.
CYRANO: No.
CHRISTIAN: No? Why not?
CYRANO: It's too soon. [*Looking at the time*] And too late.
CHRISTIAN: Sooner or later!
CYRANO: I know—sooner or later—of course you will;
   It's true. You must. What else? You're beautiful,
   She's handsome; Your four lips are pawns to fate!
   'It is written'! [*Half to himself*] It's the only book I hate.
   But at least, it is my words that—

ACT THREE

    ROXANE *appears at the balcony again.*

ROXANE: Is he gone? Who was it?
CYRANO: No-one, yes he's gone.
ROXANE: Good. Now we were—you were—talking of a …
CYRANO: Kiss! A 'kiss'—yes, of *words*, it's sweet enough—
ROXANE: No more words—they can never say as much
    As what we'll do and say in silence next.

    CHRISTIAN *is now trying to take the cue to climb.*

CYRANO: And soon, we will, in moments. Hold that breath.
    It's worth a thought—that word—that last word 'kiss'.
ROXANE: [*impatient*] Of course, but *words*, you said, are the abyss—
    Remember—'floral', 'perfumed', 'decorations',
    Barely worth the cost of circulation.
CYRANO: Let's not be hasty—that was just a thesis!
    We have to test assumptions.
CHRISTIAN: Do we? Jesus!

    CYRANO *carefully deconstructs and removes all romance from the notion, becoming increasingly bitter as things are spiralling out of control for them all at a dazzling pace.*

CYRANO: Let's define it—*kiss*—what is it, really?
    An unhygienic witness to the feelings
    Between a man and woman—or within genders!
    A war where both sides charge and then surrender.
    A crossroad where two meet and journey south!
    Two pilgrims to the 'Sermon on the Mouth'!
    A labial transaction, an endorsement;
    A pair of lips seeking reinforcement
    From another pair that they're in working order;
    An asylum vessel pleading at the border
    For a chance to come onshore, unsure of welcome;
    A cheque returned to sender; a referendum
    On the legal, civil right to vote in pairs;
    A landing on the world's most travelled stairs—

    Finally out of stamina and ideas, he borders on private despair.

    Up you go, go on— [*To himself*] Who really cares?

ROXANE: [*at the point of desperation now,* CYRANO's *effect on her almost disturbing to* CHRISTIAN] Shut up! I want you here, I want to taste you.

CYRANO: Get up there! Your prisoner awaits you.

CHRISTIAN: It doesn't seem so right now ...

CYRANO: Don't be stupid.
Take your arrow! I'll be blind as Cupid.

Forcing CHRISTIAN *up now:*

[*Belligerent*] Climb, you animal ...

CHRISTIAN *climbs. He and* ROXANE *kiss passionately.*

He's at his banquet, and at the grail he sips ...
At least I know they're my words on his lips ...

Music.

Woman—man—that blasted priest again.
[*Calling up*] Ah, hello there. Good evening. Madeleine.

ROXANE: Who is that?

CYRANO: Big brother.

ROXANE: [*unlocking lips*] Cyrano! Good evening.

CYRANO: Is Christian up there by any chance?

CHRISTIAN: [*with a show of great and terribly judged surprise*] Cyrano, is that you? Are you down there?

CYRANO: Yes—I am.
A priest is here for you, Roxane. You'd best come down.

CAPUCHIN *enters.*

CAPUCHIN: [*completely exhausted*] Sir, I have it on very good authority that Madeleine Robin lives here. Number three.

CYRANO: [*all sounds pronounced: 'an'*] Ro-bin? I thought you said Ro-din! Down next to Cézanne.

CAPUCHIN: I know, across from Paul Gauguin—I rang the bell.
He has a dog.

CYRANO: Oh, she's a lovely thing—Suzanne—isn't it?

ROXANE *enters with* CHRISTIAN.

CAPUCHIN: Madeleine Robin?

ROXANE: Call me Roxane.

CAPUCHIN, bewildered, presses on:
CAPUCHIN: A letter for you. From our revered general. Commander de Guiche.
CYRANO: De-gas?
CAPUCHIN: De Guiche! *De Guiche!*
CHRISTIAN: He dares write to you.
ROXANE: [*quieting* CHRISTIAN *who is unaware of the danger of the evening's earlier events*] Shh!
> [*Reading without* CAPUCHIN *hearing*]
> 'The drums are beating, or is that my heart?'

Good God.
> 'The regiments are ready to depart.
> They think me gone, but flouting marching orders,
> My naked body's bathed in holy waters.'

Oh. My. God.
> 'I've sent this monkey, who suspects nothing,
> To bring these news to you that he does ... bring,
> I'm coming from the moon to know you better,
> Doubt not the sun doth move, etc etc.'

Good father, this is important news for us all, from the general. Would you hear it?
> 'The drums do beat, they call our feet and hearts'

CAPUCHIN: Amen.
ROXANE: 'The regiments are ready to depart.
> I'll fight for France and follow God's good orders,
> And may my blood bleed out like holy waters!'

CAPUCHIN: God bless him.
ROXANE: 'I send this worthy monk to you tonight,
>> To marry you to Christian with all rites,
>> And ceremonies under this full moon ...'

Tiring of it a little:
> 'Enjoy your night ... I hope to see you soon.'
'General de Guiche, 5th Army Corp.'
CAPUCHIN *looks uncertain.*

'P.S. In lieu of a dowry, I give the convent two hundred and twenty francs.'

CAPUCHIN: Which is the bridegroom?

> ROXANE *and* CHRISTIAN *kiss and rush into the house.* CYRANO *is left alone outside.*
>
> *A few moments of solitude as* ROXANE *is taken from him forever. Then music.*

CYRANO: Ah, that can only be a man. And a man in the *minor* key. [*Realising*] De Guiche.

> *Knocks and calls through the door:*

Perhaps get to the vows quickly, you two.

> *And going back again, a little cruelly:*

Try to find these words, Christian—'I do'.

> *In a flurry of improvisation,* CYRANO *urgently grabs up a cloak or blanket or something to hand, hoods his face with it and hurls himself to the ground from a seemingly great height.*
>
> *As* DE GUICHE *approaches the door, the body falls before him.*

DE GUICHE: What is it? Are you hurt? Where did you come from?

CYRANO: Ah, my language! The moon!

DE GUICHE: The moon?

CYRANO: Yes, d'you know it?
What time is it here? What year?

DE GUICHE: What?

CYRANO: What year?—what century?—for that matter, what country?

DE GUICHE: [*attempting to move past*] Excuse me, do you mind if—?

CYRANO: A hundred years perhaps—or just a minute?
Did you see my descent?

DE GUICHE: From where?

CYRANO: The moon! I was in it. Where were you?

DE GUICHE: [*disinterested, a homeless madman*] On earth—now hit the road.

CYRANO: I did! But what road is it? Where am I? Give me a hint.
Ah, your face—Africa! No ... coalmining! Newcastle!

DE GUICHE: It's a mask. I'm wearing a mask.

CYRANO: Ah, Venice—the carnival in full swing. Which way do you swing?

DE GUICHE: I'm visiting a woman, excuse me.
CYRANO: A woman. A mask. A visit. Don't tell me—
 Your flirtation makes this location gay Paree!
DE GUICHE: Not so crazy after all, huh? Run along.
CYRANO: I've run far enough for one night. What a voyage!

Slapping dust off his chest and arse:

Dust in my bust and asteroids in my haemorrhoids,
Take off my boots, I'll show you Capricorns—
DE GUICHE: The moon? You're a maniac.
CYRANO: But from the zodiac. Aren't you curious?
 I think I wet myself passing Aquarius.
DE GUICHE: Get out of my way.
CYRANO: No way. It's my way or the Milky Way!
DE GUICHE: [*throwing him aside*] Another word, I'll have you arrested.
CYRANO: And searched? Oh God, I know the drill, it's heinous;
 Have you had the cavity search on Uranus?

 DE GUICHE *tries the door.*

A soldier, huh? You know, my modes of space flight could help the war.
I've invented three ways to penetrate that vast blue door we call the atmosphere.
DE GUICHE: [*taking up the challenge, after a gentle tapping on the door*] Three?
CYRANO: Three! One:
 I strip myself as naked as a candle.
 That's not quite true, I like to wear my sandals.
 I strap on sixty vials of morning dew,
 Evaporation sucks it up and sucks me too.
DE GUICHE: That's one.
CYRANO: A-two:
 Just take a magnet—big one—and a plate.
 An iron plate—you sit on this—and wait.
 When set—toss magnet—and the plate will follow,
 Keep jerking up like this and space will swallow …
 You in no time!
DE GUICHE: You're a fool.

CYRANO: But without a king to entertain. Damn that revolution!
DE GUICHE: Roxane!
CYRANO: I'm sure she heard, but let's pass time—the third?
DE GUICHE: The third.
CYRANO: [*pushing shit uphill*] Smoke rises ... I take up smoking. This one's yet to work, but I think there's a problem with the packaging.
DE GUICHE: Roxane! And which of these three interstellar idiocies got you to the moon tonight?
CYRANO: The fourth!
DE GUICHE: The fourth?
CYRANO: [*seeing the outside light illume, the wedding complete, and revealing his face in the moonlight*] Smelling salts.
[*Saluting*] Never come empty-headed to a wedding, sir.

The party exit the house to find DE GUICHE.

CHRISTIAN: [*saluting*] General.
ROXANE: My lord. Did you miss the tide?
DE GUICHE: I was held up.
CYRANO: Intergalactic traffic.
CAPUCHIN: The knot is tied, sir, at your instruction.
DE GUICHE: [*removing the orders from his pocket*] Well, the honey*moon* will suffer something of an eclipse.
[*To* CYRANO *and* CHRISTIAN] Your orders, report to the front immediately.
ROXANE: But the Cadets report to the hospital, do they not, General?
DE GUICHE: Oh, I'm afraid many of our finest will find their peace there, my lady.
To Arras, gentlemen, move out. Your company leaves tonight.

An explosive moment within the group.

ROXANE: No!
CYRANO: [*aside*] He thinks this hurts me.

> *At this, air-raid sirens howl, the shadow of a giant zeppelin overhead, a dreadful immense sound growing. Munitions begin to tear at the city at varying distances. The* DUENNA *and* RAGUENEAU *are trying to move* ROXANE *to safety,* CYRANO*'s fellow* CADETS *swarm into the square to collect he and* CHRISTIAN.

ACT THREE

DE GUICHE: Move out. *March!*

    CYRANO *pulls the lovers apart with difficulty.*

ROXANE: Protect him, Cyrano. Promise me.
CYRANO: I'll do my best.
ROXANE: Do better. Promise me he'll be safe.
CYRANO: I can't do that, Roxane.
ROXANE: Be his brother, as you've been mine.
CYRANO: Swords of grass won't help us in Arras, my sister.
ROXANE: Keep him warm, make sure he eats.
CYRANO: He'll have to look after himself, Roxane.
ROXANE: [*beyond desperation*] Then promise me he'll write.
CYRANO: [*stopping, saluting at attention*] Now, that I can promise. Goodnight.

    The enormous groan of the zeppelin shudders overhead. ROXANE *is motionless beneath her window.*

END OF ACT THREE

ACT FOUR

THE SEIGE OF ARRAS

A depleted and starved post, occupied by the company of Carbon de Castel-Jaloux at the siege of Arras.

In the background an embankment across the whole stage. Beyond, a view of the plain extending to the horizon. The country covered with entrenchments. Tents. Arms strewn about, drums, etc. Day is breaking with a faint glimmer of yellow sunrise in the east. Sentinels at different points. Watch-fires.

The CADETS *of Gascony, sick and near destitute, are sleeping, wrapped in their mantles.* CARBON *and* LE BRET *are keeping watch. They are very pale and thin.* CHRISTIAN *sleeps in the foreground among the others in his cloak, his face illuminated by the fire. Silence with intermittent, distant gunfire.*

Both CARBON *and* LE BRET *are emptying the remains of a series of tins and fishing for food inside,* LE BRET *trying to catch a cockroach.*

LE BRET: There's nothing.
CARBON: Not a morsel.
LE BRET: This is intolerable.
CARBON: Only if you can't tolerate it.
LE BRET: [*hurling the tins*] Mordioux!
CARBON: Curse quietly. You'll wake them.
 [*To a* CADET] Shh! Sleep on.
 [*To* LE BRET] When they sleep, they dine.
LE BRET: What on?
CARBON: Memories. Of dinners past.
LE BRET: Well, that's a sorry comfort for the sleepless …

 Firing is heard in the distance.

CARBON: God damn those guns. They'll wake my sons.

 Firing is again heard, nearer this time.

LE BRET: This war would be a fine thing if it weren't for those guns.

FIRST CADET: [*moving*] Not again.
CARBON: Sleep. It's nothing!
FIRST CADET: Not reveille yet?
LE BRET: Just the usual crack at Cyrano coming back!

Those who have lifted up their heads prepare to sleep again.

SENTINEL: [*offstage*] *Ventrebleu!* Who goes there?
CYRANO: [*offstage*] Bergerac.
SENTINEL: [*offstage*] Halt! Who goes there?
CYRANO: [*offstage*] Bergerac.
SENTINEL: [*offstage*] Halt! Who goes there?
CYRANO: [*appearing at the top*] Bergerac, idiot!

CYRANO *comes in.* LE BRET *advances anxiously to meet him.*

LE BRET: Thank God—Cyrano.
CYRANO: [*making signs that he should not awake the others*] Shh!
LE BRET: You hit?
CYRANO: Never. It's become a pastime to miss me. Did you miss me?
LE BRET: They won't miss forever.
CYRANO: They're making a good fist of it. Perhaps it's illegal to shoot rhinoceros in these parts.
LE BRET: Idiot. Risking your life before breakfast to send a letter!
CARBON: Before breakfast, after breakfast—not much difference when there is no breakfast.
CYRANO: [*stopping before* CHRISTIAN] I promised he'd write often.

He looks at him.

Starving. Suffering. Filthy. But still handsome!
LE BRET: Have you told her he'll die of hunger?
CYRANO: No, never. But I do come bearing news.
CARBON: Then why not come bearing provisions?
CYRANO: I have to travel light to pass the Prussian lines. [*Quietly to* LE BRET, *not wanting to raise speculative panic*] But something's afoot. There'll be a surprise for us tonight I fear. Tomorrow, we'll eat or die … if I mistake not!
LE BRET: What is it? Tell him.
CYRANO: Not yet. I could be wrong … we'll see …
CARBON: It is disgraceful that we should starve while *we're* besieging!

CYRANO: It's a complicated siege! We besiege Arras and the Prussian prince besieges us!
LE BRET: Wish someone would hurry up and besiege him!
Meanwhile, you risk a life so precious ... for the sake of a letter—

Seeing CYRANO *turning to enter the tent:*

Where are you going?
CYRANO: To write another.

CYRANO *enters the tent and disappears.*

The next morning. Day is breaking in a rosy light over the camp. The town of Arras golden on the horizon. The report of cannon is heard in the distance, followed immediately by the beating of drums far away to the left. Other drums are heard much nearer. Sounds of stirring in the camp. Voices of officers in the distance.

CARBON: [*sighing*] The reveille!

The CADETS *move and stretch themselves.*

Here comes their dawn prayer ...
FIRST CADET: [*sitting up*] Any food?
SECOND CADET: I am so hungry!
CARBON: That's enough. Rise and shine.
THIRD CADET: Rise and shine ... and die!
CARBON: Up!
THIRD CADET: I can't move.
FOURTH CADET: I'm just gonna die right here.
SECOND CADET: Be my guest.
THIRD CADET: We're all gonna die right here. Make no mistake.
SECOND CADET: [*looking at his reflection in a piece of armour*] My tongue is yellow. Is that jaundice?
FIRST CADET: It's not cheese.
SECOND CADET: Cheese. I'd make do with a mouse this morning. My kingdom for a mouse.
FOURTH CADET: Shut up! *Shut up!*
CARBON: Boys, some dignity.
THIRD CADET: Yeah, starve with dignity, boys.
FIRST CADET: Rot with self-respect.
CARBON: [*sharply*] Gentlemen.

ACT FOUR

THIRD CADET: [*dangerously, with a shadow of mutiny*] Captain!
CARBON: You wish to speak, soldier?
THIRD CADET: I wish to eat, Captain.
CARBON: You wish to eat captain? I'd eat a colonel and work my way up to the marshal who sent us here. Sit down, soldier.
LE BRET: [*at the entrance*] Cyrano. Out here.
FOURTH CADET: Sit, Jean.
THIRD CADET: Stand, Albert. I'll die out there, sir, but not in here, with no bread in my stomach. You'll find my fossil in the field.

    THIRD CADET *exits.*

LE BRET: Cyrano.

    CYRANO *appears.*

A mutinous mutter, speak to them.
FIRST CADET: [*rushing toward another who is munching something*] Hey, what are you chewing?
FOURTH CADET: Nothing.
FIRST CADET: He's chewing something. What are you chewing?

    An instant melee proceeds over the contents of the FIRST CADET*'s mouth. The contents removed, they are examined with fervour by the* FOURTH CADET.

FOURTH CADET: Cannon wads … in axle grease! It numbs the ulcers.
CARBON: [*throwing them away*] And the mind.
CYRANO: [*very calm, with a pencil behind his ear and a book in his hand*] What's wrong, lads? I'm trying to work.

    Silence.

[*To the* SECOND CADET] Where are you going?
SECOND CADET: A walk, my leg's gone to sleep.
CYRANO: So's mine.
SECOND CADET: And my stomach!
CYRANO: Me too. There's a coincidence! Good for the figure though, isn't it? And they say heaven has narrow gates!
FOURTH CADET: Don't try to calm us with jests.
CYRANO: I could live for two weeks on a good jest. Here's one I heard passing the Prussians—
'I can't stand the French …' (Why not?) 'They give me the crêpes!'

FOURTH CADET: Cyrano, we're not children.
CYRANO: [*recognising the challenge is a real one today*] No. You're taller.
THIRD CADET: Our stomachs are empty.
CYRANO: They'd make a fine drum.
FIRST CADET: I have a strange ringing in my ears.
SECOND CADET: Me too!
LE BRET: I have a strange whinging in mine.
FIRST CADET: We're going for food. Come on.
   The CADETS *gather their things and make to move out.*
CARBON: Gascons!
CYRANO: [*throwing his helmet on the floor*] There's a salad. Just needs tossing.
   The CADETS *race to it.*
FOURTH CADET: There's no salad!
CYRANO: [*tossing a book into the helmet*] Then try the *Iliad*. Feeds the soul.
   The CADETS *revolt—one finally speaks for them all.*
THIRD CADET: Why do we accept a miserable death, here, in this hell, with not a seed in our guts—
SECOND CADET: I'd rather put a bullet there—
THIRD CADET: While the cardinal, the marshal, the politicians that sent us here, guzzle away at six meals a day in Paris?
CYRANO: Is that a rhetorical question?
THIRD CADET: I want an answer.
CYRANO: I'll order you one. *Serveur!*
FIRST CADET: Always scoring a point. A clever phrase.
CYRANO: [*taking up a sword and displaying the tip*] You won't find a point in my heart without a point on my lips.
THIRD CADET: [*crying out*] We're hungry!
LE BRET: [*exploding with immense rage*] The whole world is hungry! Can you think only of yourselves?
CYRANO: Bertrand the piper—you were a shepherd once—
   Share with us the air we used to breathe,
   Draw your breath to blow a breeze through these
   Greedy guzzlers who forget the south,

ACT FOUR

Music begins.

The kingdom of their youth, their homes; I doubt
They can recall the smoke of cottage fires,
The echoed dear-home voices; rising spires
Of the churches; the bending roofs that cluster;

They listen in silence.

These notes—they call us like a little sister.
Don't they? They call us home for sunset dinners,
Our mothers out on porches calling winners
And losers from their games and treasures,
'We'll play again tomorrow', say the leaders.
A lazy melody … yet it ascends.
Creeps up on men who know they face their ends,
No longer children, playing games, and free,
Always innocence, always victory.
His flute is now a warrior, a fife,
But those fingers can still dance an older life.
Listen, boys—it no longer calls to combat.
It's a love song, it's the river in Armagnac.
It's the sunburn, it's the carousel in Riez,
It's the music in our bloods, it's Gascony.

The CADETS sit with bowed heads; tears wiped on cuffs and cloaks.

CARBON: [*to* CYRANO *quietly*] But you make them weep!
CYRANO: Homesick is better than hungry. A nobler pain.
CARBON: You'll weaken their will to fight.
CYRANO: [*taking up a drum*] You think?

He beats the drum.

ALL CADETS: [*as they stand and rush to take arms*] What? What is it?
CYRANO: [*his point proven*] I'll be in my suite!
FOURTH CADET: Here comes General de Guiche.

Muttering, groans, loathing.

THIRD CADET: Look at him, clean as a whistle.
FIRST CADET: He makes me sick.
CARBON: And yet he too is a Gascon.
SECOND CADET: Ay, a false Gascon. He's too sane to be a Gascon.

FOURTH CADET: That's why he's so dangerous.
LE BRET: He's as pale as we are.
CARBON: He's hungry too, I guess.
FIRST CADET: Oh! He's hungry! Just like us, is he? Let him eat one of his stars—
LE BRET: Let it go. Don't let him see us suffer. Get out your cards, your dice …

> *All begin spreading out the games on the drums, the stools, the ground, and on their cloaks, and they light long pipes.*

CYRANO: I'll read Descartes.

> *He walks reading a book which he has drawn from his pocket. Tableau.*

> DE GUICHE *enters. All appear absorbed and happy.* DE GUICHE *is very pale. He approaches* CARBON.

DE GUICHE: [*to* CARBON] Morning.

> *He assesses* CHRISTIAN.

He's sick.
CARBON: Well done, doctor.
DE GUICHE: So, still black looks from the Gascons, huh?
The happy few! This impressive band of buskers,
Can't endure the presence of their commander-in-chief?

> *Silence. All smoke and play.*

I thought perhaps, after the feats of yesterday,
They would boldly claim me as their own.

> *He gets a reluctant stir of interest from the group.*

Ah, you did hear of it then? While you played cards,
I lashed the Count de Bucquoi out of Bapaume,
Scattered his men, swept over them like an avalanche of stone.
I charged three times.
CYRANO: [*without lifting his eyes from his book*] And where's your white plume?
DE GUICHE: [*surprised and gratified*] Oh, you heard that too? But only half the story, I'm sure.
CARBON: The other half, my lord?

DE GUICHE: Gladly. I began the third charge and found myself caught in an eddy of deserters, driving me into the enemy lines. I was in danger of being shot—
FIRST CADET: Heaven forbid—in a war?
DE GUICHE: Or taken prisoner by a merciless foe, when I had the presence of mind to let fall the plume that marks my rank, and thereby, inconspicuous, escaped to rally reinforcements. We crushed them on the flank.

> *The* CADETS *pretend not to be listening, but the cards and the dice boxes remain suspended in their hands, the smoke of their pipes in their cheeks. They wait.*

CYRANO: That white plume wasn't yours to lose, no more than a man's soul's his own before God.
DE GUICHE: Oh? Whose was it?
CYRANO: [*an outburst*] Mine!
His! Ours! France's!
That plume is our panache. Our collective soul.
Henry of Navarre, Henry the Fourth of France
Would never lose it in his day's advance.

> *Silent delight. The cards fall, the dice rattle. The smoke is puffed.*

DE GUICHE: [*retaliating*] He would to guarantee that day's success.

> *Same suspension of play, etc.*

CYRANO: Never. Victory is defeat in hollow breasts.
I would never lightly abdicate the honour
To serve as target, even cannon fodder.
Had I been present when your feather fell,
I'd have picked it up and worn it into hell.
DE GUICHE: You vain Gascons have your boasting on tap!
CYRANO: A boast? Lend me the plume. Jean, fetch my cap.
I pledge myself, tonight, to lead the assault.

> *The* CADETS *roar.*

DE GUICHE: Another Gascon bluff! You foolish dolts,
You know the plume lies with the enemy
In no man's land—
CYRANO: And I say lend it me!

DE GUICHE: *I cannot!* Dropped in darkness! On the brink
Of chaos, mud and blood all riddled pink.
No-one can lend it you, their line of fire
Laces the riverbank. And razor wire;
Understand! The plume is gone, and where it lies
No-one could fetch it and return alive.
CYRANO: [*drawing the plume from his pocket, and holding it out to him, while turning a page and not looking up*] What, this one?

    Silence. The CADETS *stifle laughter in their cards and dice boxes. One of them whistles indifferently the air just played by the fifer.*

DE GUICHE: [*taking the plume*] Thank you. This will do very well to wend
The signal I was loathe, till now, to send.

    He goes to the rampart, climbs it, and waves the plume three times.

ALL: What's that? What's he doing? He's waving it.
SENTINEL: [*from the top of the rampart*] There's a man there, running away.
DE GUICHE: [*returning*] My Prussian spy, taking the signal with him.
CARBON: Spy?
DE GUICHE: Yes, incorrigible fellow. But extremely useful,
Gives the enemy whatever news I want them to hear.
CYRANO: Scoundrel!
CARBON: What news?
DE GUICHE: [*carelessly re-applying his plume*] The marshal has offered a plan to break this deplorable stalemate. It's promising, but not without sacrifice. The few who fall will save the many.
LE BRET: What plan?
DE GUICHE: To invite the enemy to attack our ranks at our weakest point ... where we carry fewest numbers ... Once they've cut a swathe through us and believe they can march toward Paris, we have six thousand horse will fall upon them from the woods.
CARBON: The weakest point?
DE GUICHE: [*spelling it out to the depleted troop*] Where we carry ... fewest ... numbers ...
CARBON: We are so few because we've held this garrison without reinforcement for three months.
DE GUICHE: A Gascon has the strength of many men! It's a credit to you.

ACT FOUR

CYRANO: [*gathering his arms*] When should we expect them?
DE GUICHE: They stand upon my signal.
CARBON: [*to the* CADETS] Which he just gave. Make ready!

All rise. Weapons taken up.

DE GUICHE: Within an hour, gentlemen, at fifteen hundred.
FIRST CADET: Oh, well then.

They all sit down again and take up their games.

DE GUICHE: [*leaving*] Make a good show of it, gentlemen. Die well.
CYRANO: A neat vengeance, General, I commend you.
DE GUICHE: I serve my country—
CYRANO: And your grudge as well.
DE GUICHE: You feel at home against a hundred men!
I give your friends the chance to do the same.
[*A parting shot*] Or you could always try the moon.

DE GUICHE *exits*.

CYRANO: [*to the* CADETS] Well, Gascons, let us add unto our coat of arms, a new chevron. In blood!

Orders are given. Preparations. CYRANO *goes to* CHRISTIAN.

[*Putting his hand on* CHRISTIAN*'s shoulder*] Christian!
CHRISTIAN: Roxane!
CYRANO: I know.
CHRISTIAN: I want you to say everything that's in my heart … in a way that she will never forget. A last letter.
CYRANO: I know.
CHRISTIAN: I want to say goodbye.
CYRANO: I know. I have.

He removes the letter from his coat.

CHRISTIAN: Let me see it.
CYRANO: You want to … read it?
CHRISTIAN: Yes.
CYRANO: Right. [*Almost handing it over*] Why?
CHRISTIAN: Because I wrote it …
CYRANO: Of course.

CHRISTIAN *reads. Taken with something, he examines it.*

CHRISTIAN: What's this spot? This circle?
CYRANO: Dirt. A smudge of ink.
CHRISTIAN: No it's not. It's a tear!
CYRANO: [*with as much innocence as he can muster, deliberately mishearing the word for its namesake—a 'tear' or 'rip'*] A tear? Where?
CHRISTIAN: A tear!
CYRANO: Tear. Really? Oh, yeah … a poet has to feel …
  Whatever he's imagining is real.
  Writing this letter for you while you slept,
  The words became a part of me—
CHRISTIAN: You wept?
CYRANO: Well … death itself … is not so terrible.
  Not to see her again … that's unbearable.
  I may never—we may never—you may …

> CHRISTIAN *stares at him.* CYRANO *takes the letter back. Shots far off in the camp.*

SENTINEL: [*offstage*] Who goes there?!

> *Shots. Voices. Carriage bells.*

CARBON: What is it?
SENTINEL: [*on the rampart*] A carriage!

> *All rush to see.*

VOICES: In the camp?!
  It's not ours!—Fire!—No!—Hold your fire!
  What does he say?!—'For the Gascons!'

> *Everyone is on the rampart, staring. The carriage comes nearer.*

DE GUICHE: [*re-entering*] For the Gascons? How? What is it?

> *All descend and draw up in line. The carriage enters at full speed, covered with dust and mud. The curtains are drawn close. It is pulls up suddenly.*

CARBON: Beat a salute!

> *A roll of drums. The* CADETS *are poised to fire.*

DE GUICHE: Stand forth.

> *Two* CADETS *rush forward. The hatch opens.*

ACT FOUR

ROXANE: [*revealed*] Hello, boys!
DE GUICHE: You?
ROXANE: Me.
CYRANO: My God.
CHRISTIAN: [*rushing forward*] What are you doing here?
ROXANE: This siege ... is too long!
CHRISTIAN: But why ...?
DE GUICHE: You cannot be here!
ROXANE: [*merrily*] But I can! And I am. And now, I need a hand. Anyone?

Finally, a CADET *aids her descent.*

Thank you, sir.
[*Proudly*] My carriage was fired at by a patrol!
[*Kissing* CHRISTIAN *simply*] Husband!
[*Examining them all*] Why so sad, you lot? Did I come at a bad time?
DE GUICHE: [*quietly*] The worst.
CYRANO: [*coming up to her*] But how, in God's name, did you—
ROXANE: Find my way? It was simple enough, I followed the waste, I knew, big brother, [*to* CYRANO] that where the war was worst, there you'd be.
CYRANO: But this is madness! How did you get through ...?
ROXANE: The enemy lines? Easy really, I just smiled. I don't mean to disparage the French, but those Prussians are the most gallant on earth, such courtesy. All I had to say was, 'I go to find my lover' and their hearts opened wider than their gates.
CHRISTIAN: But, Roxane ...
DE GUICHE: You have to leave this place!
ROXANE: I just arrived.
CYRANO: Now!
LE BRET: Now, Roxane.
CHRISTIAN: Go.
ROXANE: Why?
CHRISTIAN: [*embarrassed*] Because ...
CYRANO: In three quarters of an hour ...
DE GUICHE: More or less ...
CARBON: It'd be best if—ah—
LE BRET: [*leading her away*] Roxane ...

ROXANE: You are going to fight—You're going to fight! I'm staying here.
ALL: No, no!
ROXANE: He is my husband!

She throws herself into CHRISTIAN's *arms.*

We die together.
FIRST CADET: We'll defend you to the death.
ROXANE: Oh ... thank you. But I don't fear to die. I come of courageous stock.

She looks at her cousin, then turns her glare upon DE GUICHE.

But perhaps the time has come for the Count to be discreet and beat a retreat. The fighting may start soon!
DE GUICHE: I go to inspect the guns. When I return, you will be gone, Roxane.
ROXANE: Is that an order?
DE GUICHE: It's a request.

DE GUICHE *exits.*

ROXANE: Never!
CHRISTIAN: [*desperate*] Roxane!
ROXANE: No!
THIRD CADET: [*to the others*] She stays!

All the CADETS *hurry, hustling each other, tidying themselves.*

CARBON, *who, like the others, has been buckling, dusting, brushing his hat, settling his plume, and drawing on his cuffs, advances to* ROXANE *and ceremoniously takes her by the arm.*

CARBON: Madame, may I then present to you these gentlemen, who have the honour of dying, bravely, in your presence.

ROXANE *bows and, on his arm, is introduced.*

Baron de Peyrescous de Colignac!
FIRST CADET [*with a low reverence*] Madame ...
CARBON: [*continuing*] Baron Jean de Casterac de Cahuzac,
    Vidame Le Bret de Malgouyre Estressac Lesbas d'Escarabiot,
    Chevalier Albert d'Antignac-Juzet,
    Baron Hillot de Blagnac-Salechan de Castel Crabioules ...
ROXANE: Your signatures must be exhausting.

ACT FOUR

CARBON: If you would open your hand, madame.
ROXANE: [*opening her hand, her handkerchief falls*] Why?
 The whole company start forward to pick it up.
CARBON: [*quickly raising it*] My company had no flag. Now we have the finest in the camp!
ROXANE: It's a bit small.
 Awed by its delicacy, its reminder of Parisian life, the SECOND CADET, *almost in tears, is tying the handkerchief on a pike.*
SECOND CADET: But made of lace!
ROXANE: Good. Well, I am famished. Some paté, a pastry, cold chicken, and some wine—would do me nicely. Thank you.
 Consternation.
CHRISTIAN: Roxane.
ROXANE: Oh—and a crème brûlée. The lot, please. Who'll carve and serve? And we'll need to reheat the sauce.
CYRANO: Roxane.
ROXANE: Does nobody recognise my coachman?!
 Silence.
RAGUENEAU: Gentlemen …!
CADETS: Ragueneau!
ROXANE: [*looking after them*] Poor boys!
CYRANO: [*kissing her hand*] An angel.
 General delight.
CADETS: Bravo! bravo!
RAGUENEAU: The Prussians, gazing on so fair a dainty, overlooked such dainty fare …!
 Applause as he reveals a banquet.
CYRANO: [*urgently trying to isolate* CHRISTIAN] Christian! A word.
RAGUENEAU: While motioning Venus on, they overlooked the venison!
 Enthusiasm. Twenty hands are held out to seize the shoulder of mutton.
CYRANO: I need to speak to you!
ROXANE: Lay it out, boys.

The CADETS *come down, their arms laden with food.*

[*To* CHRISTIAN, *just as* CYRANO *is drawing him apart*] Come, make yourself useful!

CHRISTIAN *comes to help.* CYRANO*'s uneasiness increases.*

RAGUENEAU: Truffled peacock. These lanterns hold more precious gifts than light!

CYRANO: I need to talk to you before you talk to her. Christian.

RAGUENEAU: [*throwing down the carriage cushions*] Cushions! Stuffed with cuisine!

They inspect the contents of the cushions. Bursts of laughter etc.

FOURTH CADET: Ah! *Viédaze!*

RAGUENEAU *throws down disguised bottles of red wine to the* CADETS.

RAGUENEAU: Flasks of rubies!— [*And white wine*] Flasks of topaz!

CARBON: Where's de Guiche?

THIRD CADET: None for him. Let him starve.

CARBON: Manners, boys!

ROXANE *throws a folded tablecloth at* CYRANO*'s head.*

ROXANE: Unfold me that napkin!—Come, on! Join us, cousin.
[*To* SECOND CADET] Don't eat too fast. You have time enough! Here, drink a little—
Why are you crying?

SECOND CADET: It's just so good …!

ROXANE: Rare praise, Ragueneau!—Red or white?—Some bread for Monsieur de Carbon!—A knife! Pass your plate!—A little of the crust? Some more? Let me help you!—Some champagne?—A wing?

CYRANO: How I worship her!

ROXANE: [*going up to* CHRISTIAN] And what for you, my love?

CHRISTIAN: Nothing.

ROXANE: No, take this—

CHRISTIAN: Tell me why you came?

ROXANE: Duty first! To feed these fellows.

LE BRET *has gone up to pass a loaf of bread on the end of a lance to the* SENTRY *on the rampart.*

LE BRET: De Guiche!
CARBON: Quick! Hide flasks, plates, dishes, Ragueneau, everything!—Act normal.

> DE GUICHE *enters hurriedly. Stops suddenly, sniffing the air.*
> *Silence.*

DE GUICHE: What smells good? You've changed colour.
THIRD CADET: The breeze.
DE GUICHE: [*looking at him*] What is the matter?—You're red.
THIRD CADET: Nothing ... blood ... boiling ... battle—

> FIRST CADET, *a little pissed, sings something—perhaps whistling Bertrand's song.*

DE GUICHE: [*turning around*] What's that?
FIRST CADET: It's a song!—A little ... song.
DE GUICHE: What are you happy about?
FOURTH CADET: Danger ... it's intoxicating!
DE GUICHE: [*calling* CARBON *to give him an order*] Captain! I ... you look unnaturally healthy.
CARBON: [*crimson in the face, hiding a bottle*] A happy oblivion, my lord.
DE GUICHE: I have one cannon left, and have had it carried there— [*pointing behind the scenes*] use it as you need.
FIRST CADET: [*pissed*] It's a charming cannon!
DE GUICHE: [*quickly to* ROXANE] Madame, your decision?
ROXANE: I'm here to stay.
DE GUICHE: You cannot.
ROXANE: But I can.
DE GUICHE: Then give me a musket, one of you!
CARBON: What for?
DE GUICHE: I won't desert a lady.
CYRANO: Our weakest point!
FIRST CADET: [*genuinely*] Then you are a Gascon after all?

> *Delight from the* CADETS. DE GUICHE *surprised by his own pride. A* CADET *uncovers the feast.*

DE GUICHE: [*eyes sparkling*] Victuals!
SECOND CADET: Troops appearing on the ridge, sir.

Taking DE GUICHE's *meal before he can touch a spoil, they go up toward the rampart. All follow.*

CHRISTIAN: [*going to* CYRANO, *eagerly*] Tell me quickly! What is it?
CYRANO: Just in case Roxane …
CHRISTIAN: Yes …?
CYRANO: You may find she mentions—
CHRISTIAN: A letter. Yes.
CYRANO: Not *a* letter … letters—
CHRISTIAN: [*moving off*] Yes, I know! …
CYRANO: Just—don't look too surprised …
CHRISTIAN: [*exasperated*] At what?
CYRANO: Well, I'm explaining it to you! … It's no big deal.
  I just thought it may be time … I should reveal …
CHRISTIAN: Reveal what? Tell me quickly.
CYRANO: I am! Listen, kid,
  You wrote … more often than you think you did.
CHRISTIAN: I did?
CYRANO: Look, I had a job to do, a mandate, a commission,
  To express your love—without express permission.
  I devoted a bit of time to—correspondence.
  I didn't tell you—you were so despondent,
  And …
CHRISTIAN: But we're cut off, how did you get them through?
CYRANO: Oh! Before the dawn … I was able to …
CHRISTIAN: [*the first tremors of revelation*] Oh, and that was simple enough? How many times?
CYRANO: Um …
CHRISTIAN: How often in a month? … a week …?
CYRANO: My rhymes …? Um …
CHRISTIAN: Yes. Once or twice?
CYRANO: A little more than that.
CHRISTIAN: What! Once a week?
CYRANO: If I was feeling flat.
CHRISTIAN: And if you were feeling good?
CYRANO: To be precise?
  In a day … I think … I usually wrote her twice.
CHRISTIAN: Twice a day. You wrote her twice a day?

ACT FOUR

CYRANO: Mostly, yes—I once got three away.
CHRISTIAN: [*with a degree of revelation/discovery/violence*] And what would make you brave your death for me?
You crossed the lines each day? ... Oh, now I see.
CYRANO: [*seeing* ROXANE *returning*] Not now, not in front of her.

> CYRANO *goes hurriedly into his tent.*
>
> *In the distance* CADETS *coming and going.* CARBON *and* DE GUICHE *give orders.*

ROXANE: [*running up to* CHRISTIAN] Ah, Christian, at last ...!

> *She throws a white sash scarf she has knitted around his neck.*

CHRISTIAN: Now tell me why you're here. Why would you risk this?
ROXANE: For you, for love. Your letters.
CHRISTIAN: That's not possible.
ROXANE: It's your fault. Your letters were a daily ecstasy.
These many months, so many words, each more surprising than the last!
CHRISTIAN: What!—For a few letters, you would ...
ROXANE: I would. I have. Those words divined my soul.
CHRISTIAN: What words, exactly?
ROXANE: You don't recognise your genius, do you?
CHRISTIAN: Perhaps not. What words?
ROXANE: The ones you spoke to me that summer evening,
A voice I'd never known—among the jasmine—
A love that I could never have imagined.

> CHRISTIAN *is almost unable to stand.*

Don't be embarrassed! I know it was the darkness,
A man must seek such anonymity,
To reveal his truest self, or the proximity
Of pen and ink and time and long distance.
Your siege of words that night broke my resistance,
I loved you then, I thought I did before—
But superficially, skin-deep, childish amour—

> *Opening a chest on the cart:*

Your daily song was sung in that same voice.

Pouring an untold number of letters over him, in rapture:

These lit my way to you, I had no choice.
Penelope would not have sat and weaved,
In patience if Ulysses had conceived,
Of such a manifesto, such rare blisses,
She would have come—to coat his arms in kisses.

CHRISTIAN: Roxane …

ROXANE: [*slowly between kisses, a physical need for him*] I read—and read—and re-read your temerity,
At night, at morn, in bed, your bold sincerity—

CHRISTIAN: Sincerity! You believe the love sincere?

ROXANE: *Sans question*, luminous, a chandelier
Ablaze in every page, words scorched with truth.

CHRISTIAN: And so you came.

ROXANE: I came, and more than once!

CHRISTIAN: Roxane!

ROXANE: [*ironic, selflessly modern*] I know, I'm so ashamed! I'm truly not,

Finding a specific reference in one letter, she shows him.

You said you'd 'take no prisoners'—

CHRISTIAN: Yes—I forgot.

ROXANE: And this phrase!

She shows him another. He stares it through.

You know you *sentenced* me with this!
I am ashamed of one thing, I confess.
Forgive me for the shallowness I've shown,
At first I loved your beauty. That alone.

CHRISTIAN: And now?

ROXANE: Alas, you've wreaked your own downfall!
I see you—yet I don't see you at all.
I feel you now. I know you truly. Whole.
Flesh and body yes, but more—your soul …
I love—

CHRISTIAN: My soul? I'm happy with the flesh,
Go back to that, I never asked for this.

ROXANE: For what?

ACT FOUR

CHRISTIAN: For love—like this—so complicated.
ROXANE: [*chastising him with some vehemence*] Men and women never
   do. That's why they're fated
   To eternally neglect and fail each other,
   Infidelitous and specious; else they smother
   Love with empty kindnesses and customs,
   Placid and decorous; let's soar above them.
CHRISTIAN: [*despairing now*] I don't want to. I want to love—usually;
   Like normal people do, just—normally.
ROXANE: [*misreading, playful again*] Okay, I promise, I'll let your looks—distract me,
   From time to time, though your books attract me;
   On Tuesdays and Thursdays we'll 'play dumb',
   An if we live now through the hour to come—
CHRISTIAN: I never said 'play dumb'! Why can't you love me
   For who I am, I don't want to—soar above me …
   Love me for my looks, I'm not offended—
ROXANE: [*streaming with consciousness now*] Oh, like others have I'm sure, a never-ending
   Stream of heads have turned your way to gaze
   At beauty, underestimating ways
   Your mind would dazzle them if they'd dare look
   Within—so I refuse to join the flock
   That 'picture' you, I'm blind to that. Eyes fail …
   To read the soul … in here [*picking up the letters*] I find the braille
   That gives your face, and flesh, its true perspective.
   In fact, I dare think I'd not be protective
   Of your beauty if it now suffered loss,
   If you were ugly, dwarfish, twisted, gross.
CHRISTIAN: Don't say that—
ROXANE: Listen, Christian, I adore …
   You. Less handsome? I'd only love you more.
CHRISTIAN: My God!
   Beat.
   If I were ugly …?
ROXANE: [*enjoying the prospect*] *Deformed!* Are you happy now?
CHRISTIAN: Yes. I am.

ROXANE: What's wrong?
CHRISTIAN: [*gently pushing her away*] Nothing ... Go and cheer those boys before they fight.
I need a second, just a minute on my own.
ROXANE: My Christian ...!

> *She goes up to the* CADETS, *who respectfully crowd around her as she talks to them and* CARBON.
>
> CHRISTIAN *and* CYRANO *come forward.*

CHRISTIAN: [*calling toward* CYRANO'*s tent*] Cyrano!
CYRANO: [*reappearing, fully armed*] What? Why so pale?
CHRISTIAN: She doesn't love me!
CYRANO: What?
CHRISTIAN: She loves you.
CYRANO: What?
CHRISTIAN: She only loves me for my soul.
CYRANO: Really?—I mean—What?
CHRISTIAN: You are my soul.

> *Silence.*

CYRANO: Don't be an idiot.
CHRISTIAN: You love her too.

> *Beat.*

Don't say 'what?'.
Do you?
I know you do.
CYRANO: It's true.
CHRISTIAN: Madly.
CYRANO: More.
CHRISTIAN: Tell her.
CYRANO: No!
CHRISTIAN: Why not?
CYRANO: Because.
CHRISTIAN: Why not?
CYRANO: Look at me!
CHRISTIAN: She doesn't care. In fact, she'd prefer it.
CYRANO: Prefer what?

CHRISTIAN: If I were ... she'd only love me more.
CYRANO: Don't believe that, that's not—
CHRISTIAN: It is. She loves you.
  I won't destroy your happiness anymore.
CYRANO: [*deeply affected by this*] She said so? If you were ugly ...?
CHRISTIAN: The very words.
CYRANO: No, she doesn't mean that. I won't destroy *your* happiness ...
CHRISTIAN: [*going to get her*] Then she'll choose between us.
CYRANO: No! no! Spare me that!
CHRISTIAN: Tell her!
CYRANO: No.
CHRISTIAN: I won't be my own rival anymore. I'm a nonentity, are you too stupid to see?
  I know what I am—and I'll be loved for that—or not at all.
CYRANO: This whole conversation—though dramatic—is academic. We're both going to die.
CHRISTIAN: No, you must live. [*Calling*] Roxane!
  Tell her. Let her choose.
CYRANO: I know what her choice will be—You.

  Beat as ROXANE *comes forward.*

CHRISTIAN: I hope so.
  Cyrano has something to say.
ROXANE: I think I've upset him. I said something ...
CYRANO: I know what you said. Say it again. Even if he were ugly ...?

  Gunfire as the battle begins.

  Roxane. Even if he were ...
ROXANE: Even then, of course. It's begun—Cyrano.
CYRANO: Terribly ugly? Twisted? Grotesque? Deformed?
ROXANE: All the more. Cyrano, the war.
CYRANO: You swear you'd love him.
ROXANE: Evermore.
CYRANO: My God. Is it possible?
  Roxane, listen to me ...

    LE BRET *enters.*

LE BRET: [*seeing* ROXANE, *speaking to* CYRANO *alone, in his ear*]
  Cyrano.

CYRANO: No. No.
ROXANE: What? What's happening?
CYRANO: Roxane.
ROXANE: What is it? You were telling me something ...
CYRANO: Something? Yes. Never now ...
ROXANE: *What is it?*
CYRANO: Christian. It's over ...

    CHRISTIAN *is carried on, bloodied, dying.*

ROXANE: Christian! Christian.
LE BRET: He was first over the parapet.
FIRST CADET: The first shot.

    CARBON *enters.*

CARBON: [*seeing the need to carry on*] Gentlemen! They're attacking! Man the cannon!
ROXANE: Christian!

    RAGUENEAU *briefly manages to extract her from the sight.*

CYRANO: I told her everything, Christian.
It's you she loves.
CHRISTIAN: Roxane.
CARBON: [*offstage*] Measure your fire line. Steady. Set. Fire!
ROXANE: My love.
CYRANO: He has a letter ...
CARBON: [*offstage*] Charge!
ROXANE: He's not dead. He's not dead. Christian. Speak. My love. *Help me!*
CYRANO: Roxane—I must go. They need me.
ROXANE: Stay. He's dead. You were his friend. He's dead.
CYRANO: Yes.
ROXANE: You knew his greatness, no-one knew.
CYRANO: Yes, Roxane.
ROXANE: He was a great soul, wasn't he? Wasn't he?
CYRANO: Yes, Roxane.
ROXANE: A genius—no end to his magnificence—his tenderness.
CYRANO: Yes, Roxane.
ROXANE: He's gone.

ACT FOUR

DE GUICHE: [*offstage*] The signal. Hold, boys. Reinforcements coming now. Hold the line.

CYRANO: [*aside*] I must die. In weeping him, she already mourns for me.

ROXANE: [*to* RAGUENEAU] There are tears on his letter—tears and blood. His brave blood, his perfect tears ... look at this circle.

CADETS: Gascony!

CYRANO: [*to the wounded* DE GUICHE] Get her away.

DE GUICHE: No, you. I'll fight.

CYRANO: Get her away, my lord. I'll lead the charge. Go, *go!* Goodbye, Roxane.

CARBON enters, shaken, with others.

CARBON: We have to fall back.

CHRISTIAN's body is dumped on the cart and begins its journey.

CYRANO: [*wild*] *Reculez pas!* Hardi! Drollos!
Fly this little flag and fight, my boys, my Gascons!
Tombe dessus. Escrasus tous! Play your pipes!

SECOND CADET: They're coming over!

CARBON: Fire!

Cannon.

Fire!

Cannon.

CYRANO: We are the Gascony Cadets!
Of Captain de Castel Jaloux
Braggers of brags and layers of bets,
We are the Gascony Cadets.
We'll fight, we'll die,
By land and sea ...

Drowned out by battle, the flag of the enemy appears. The CADETS *make their final charge, their song on their lips.*

END OF ACT FOUR

ACT FIVE

CYRANO'S GAZETTE

Fifteen years later, early 1930s. Park of the Sisters of the Holy Cross in Paris. An enormous plane tree in the middle of the stage, standing alone. On the left, a semicircular stone bench. A broken gate deep in the distance.

A mass of autumn leaves. Two chairs. Baskets full of skeins and balls of wool beside Roxane's empty garden chair. Lying over the chair, and stretching as far as the stage allows and further yet, is a scarf she has been knitting—white. It is scarf she had brought to Christian in Arras. She has been knitting it for nearly fifteen years.

At the rising of the curtain, SISTER MARTHA *and* SISTER CLAIRE *are working the untidy garden;* MOTHER MARGUERITE *(Mother Superior) sits in a chair. Leaves are falling.*

SISTER MARTHA: [*to* MOTHER MARGUERITE] Vanity is a sin, isn't it, Holy Mother?

MOTHER MARGUERITE: A mortal one.

SISTER MARTHA: On a scale of one to ten, how *bad*?

MOTHER MARGUERITE: God counts souls, Sister Martha, not degrees.

SISTER MARTHA: But … bad?

MOTHER MARGUERITE: Very.

SISTER MARTHA: [*a rapid disclosure*] Sister Claire spent ten minutes doing her hair in the reflection of Brother Pierre's new coffee apparatus.

MOTHER MARGUERITE: Coffee is also a sin, Claire.

SISTER CLAIRE: A sin?

MOTHER MARGUERITE: And so is Brother Pierre.

SISTER CLAIRE: How does gluttony compare?

MOTHER MARGUERITE: Unpardonable.

SISTER CLAIRE: Sister Martha ate seven plums during Lent.

MOTHER MARGUERITE: [*genuinely a little shocked*] It is a fast, Sister Martha.

SISTER MARTHA: I ate them fast.

ACT FIVE

SISTER CLAIRE: Which of us is worse, Mother Marguerite?
SISTER MARTHA: More *bad*?
MOTHER MARGUERITE: Damnation is not an Olympiad.
SISTER CLAIRE: What is our punishment, Holy Mother?
SISTER MARTHA: Will you tell Monsieur de Bergerac?
MOTHER MARGUERITE: I'm afraid I must!
SISTER CLAIRE: Tell him about the / coffee first!
SISTER MARTHA: The plums I ate.
SISTER CLAIRE: Eight? It was only seven.
MOTHER MARGUERITE: He will mock you mercilessly.

A hopeful silence from the girls.

You crave the attentions of Monsieur Cyrano, Sisters?
SISTER CLAIRE & SISTER MARTHA: [*together*] She does!
MOTHER MARGUERITE: He will be here soon, you can make your *confessions* then.
SISTER MARTHA: He's not a ... model ... Catholic, is he, Holy Mother?
MOTHER MARGUERITE: You won't find him in the manuals ...
SISTER CLAIRE: Do you fear for his soul, Mother?
MOTHER MARGUERITE: I pray for it.
SISTER MARTHA: We'll convert him!
MOTHER MARGUERITE: [*with severity*] Never. Leave him be!
If we meddle with his mortal soul, he may ... stop coming.
SISTER CLAIRE: He told me last week that he only breaks rules he's supposed to follow.
SISTER MARTHA: And that ... [*trying to recall his precise phrase*] ... if the Good Book is a guide to the afterlife, he's after a guide to the good life ...
MOTHER MARGUERITE: Well, Sisters, the Good Book is not the only book, but its rules are good enough for you. Monsieur de Bergerac will never return to the fold if he thinks we are sinners.

ROXANE has entered unseen.

ROXANE: He'll never return to the fold if he thinks you're saints!
SISTER CLAIRE: Is he here, Madame Madeleine?
ROXANE: You know he never comes until four.
SISTER MARTHA: He's been coming since I was a novice, that's seven years, and he's never missed a Saturday.

MOTHER MARGUERITE: And for seven years before that, Martha. He's visited our poor convent at four o'clock on Saturdays for fourteen years. And he's never early.
ROXANE: He's very regular, while being very irregular.
SISTER CLAIRE: I think he likes our vows—he says a life of celibacy takes 'pastiche'!
ROXANE: Panache, Claire.
SISTER CLAIRE: [*tackling* SISTER MARTHA'*s derisive laughter*] Panache ... alright, panache.
SISTER MARTHA: Pastiche! Pastiche is a type of nut, Claire.
MOTHER MARGUERITE: Pistachio, Martha.

    SISTER CLAIRE *cannot contain her joy.*

Pastiche is a form of imitation—
ROXANE: [*moving toward the back to gather something and glance toward the entrance*] And you could never accuse Cyrano of that!
SISTER MARTHA: He comes because he likes our cakes.
MOTHER MARGUERITE: He comes because ... he is the only one who can make her smile.

    A figure enters.

SISTER CLAIRE: He's here early!

    It is DE GUICHE.

MOTHER MARGUERITE: It's the Duke, ladies.
ROXANE: It must be that time of year.
DE GUICHE: Madame Madeleine. Sisters.
ROXANE: My lord. Another year has passed already?
DE GUICHE: A long time. I'm sorry, I've been busy. And here you remain, a rose distilled.
And still so fair.
ROXANE: And still so faithful.
DE GUICHE: I know it.

    Silence.

And for me, have you found ... forgiveness?
ROXANE: I have found solace.
DE GUICHE: Will you mourn forever?
ROXANE: And ever.

ACT FIVE

DE GUICHE: Was he so rare a being?
ROXANE: When you knew him well.
DE GUICHE: I suppose I never had time to tell.
ROXANE: [*sharply*] Nor did I.
DE GUICHE: Madame—I'm sorr—

> *The 3:45 bells drown his apology, twice. An awkward silence while they await them to finish.*

And his last letter, you still wear it about your heart.
ROXANE: Around about there, yes.
DE GUICHE: Even gone, you love him.
ROXANE: *He* is gone, his love is not. It surrounds me here, somehow. Christian is dead, but I sometimes feel his love is still …
DE GUICHE: And Cyrano, he still calls?
ROXANE: Like clockwork. I don't even have to turn around. Four strikes of the bell, four taps on the path—his cane tells me the time, never early, never late, he slips into that armchair and begins his *Gazette*.
DE GUICHE: His *Gazette*?
ROXANE: Yes, I still subscribe. But Cyrano's version is a little juicier than most. News, gossip, rumour, humour … satires on the court and power. Like Penelope, I stitch while he talks.

> LE BRET *entering urgently, calling.*

LE BRET: Madame Madeleine!
ROXANE: Monsieur Le Bret. How is our friend?
LE BRET: Bad. Terrible.

> *He sees* DE GUICHE *for the first time in many years. There is no time to deal with the emotional fallout of that now.*

My lord!
[*To* ROXANE] Is he here?
ROXANE: Not till four.
DE GUICHE: Terrible?
LE BRET: Worse.
ROXANE: He always exaggerates. Cyrano worsens by the week, but on Saturdays at four, he arrives at his peak!
LE BRET: For you, Madame, yes.
DE GUICHE: Does he make enemies?

LE BRET: Religiously. Nobles, hypocrites, cowards, rakes; plagiarists, heroes, literati, *fakes*—all of them. But it's not them I fear. It's older enemies—loneliness, misery, hunger— [*taking in the sky and the encroaching end to autumn*] winter.

ROXANE: He's a man for all seasons, don't diminish him.

LE BRET: But those are the seasons that'll finish him.
He tightens his belt by a new hole each day. His new black suit has been new for twelve years.

DE GUICHE: Don't pity him.

LE BRET: My lord—

DE GUICHE: Don't pity him, Le Bret.
He's lived without compromise. He's fought for that freedom, that is his prize.

LE BRET: Freedom? With all due respect, sir—

DE GUICHE: You misunderstand me. I know, I have everything, he nothing. And yet, I would be proud to shake his hand.

ROXANE: One more minute and you may.

DE GUICHE: No, he wouldn't wish it, I mustn't stay.

ROXANE: I'll see you out.

DE GUICHE: [*suddenly, deeply troubled, needing to communicate*] I envy him. His passion, his ideals, his recalcitrance; he stands always in the light, unafraid. I am eaten away by a thousand shadows—compromises, harmless but countless; broken promises—

LE BRET: Remorse.

DE GUICHE: [*playing with the scarf* ROXANE *has been stitching*] No, nothing so simple as that. A lingering unease. I envy his ... lightness of being ... even in his distress. I carry the weight of so-called success, which is really an ever-lengthening weave of neglected ideals, regrets ... a little boy's whispered hopes ... that I stopped listening to ... goodbye.

ROXANE: So ... you too are a dreamer.

DE GUICHE: [*leaving, with* ROXANE *pursuing*] We all are. Farewell.
[*Returning suddenly*] A word, monsieur. A moment, madame.
[*Privately to* LE BRET] You are right to fear his enemies, and not just the cold. There are many that hate him, none willing to meet his face, but I heard yesterday that 'Bergerac might have an accident'.

LE BRET: Where? How?

ACT FIVE

DE GUICHE: I know not. But don't let him walk abroad. Goodbye.

Missing DE GUICHE, *and as* LE BRET *makes to leave,* RAGUENEAU *bursts in from another pathway, catching* LE BRET.

RAGUENEAU: Thank God, Le Bret.

LE BRET: Not now, old friend, I have to find Cyrano.

RAGUENEAU: You do indeed! I came to tell her …

Looking at ROXANE *at a distance, he can't find the strength.*

But I'll tell you instead. I went to visit him, I was late, I saw him leaving his house, he turned the corner, I ran after him; as he passed under a high window—it was not an accident, it can't have been—a heavy lump of wood, a great log—

LE BRET: No. Is he dead?

RAGUENEAU: Not dead, but barely alive, he's in bed. I carried him home—to that hovel—a lot of blood.

LE BRET: A doctor?

RAGUENEAU: He won't have it, he diagnosed himself.

LE BRET: With what?

RAGUENEAU: Headache.

LE BRET: Idiot!

They rush off.

ROXANE: Gentlemen. [*To* MOTHER MARGUERITE] Another drama for Ragueneau!

The bell begins.

Ah, the chair … for whom the bell tolls.

SISTER CLAIRE: It's our best.

The bell ends. ROXANE *waits and speaks to fill the emptiness.*

ROXANE: He's never been late. Incredible. Perhaps he's stealing cakes! My new skein? Any minute now. My scissors.

Silence.

Perhaps he's stealing more cakes. Strange. What could keep him—?

The cane begins to tap—a hidden relief.

SISTER CLAIRE & SISTER MARTHA: [*together*] Here he is, madame. Monsieur de Bergerac.

ROXANE: Late? After fourteen years. Or is *time* running early?
CYRANO: No, Time keeps his promise. And in keeping mine, I—idiot—got waylaid.
ROXANE: Oh? An unexpected visitor? Today has been full of them.
CYRANO: Yes.
ROXANE: Friend or foe?
CYRANO: Yes ... sorry, friend, old friend ...
ROXANE: But troublesome.
CYRANO: Tiresome.
ROXANE: I hope you sent him on his way.
CYRANO: [*as a* SISTER *comes to relieve him of his hat*] Yes, I said, 'Now listen, this is Saturday, my mad-hatter day, the only-day-that-matters day. Please push off,' I said ... 'and ... ah ... come back in an hour'.
ROXANE: Well, he'll have to wait longer, I'm keeping you till evening.
CYRANO: Oh, he may ... be a little more impatient than that.

> *Expectant* SISTERS. *A feigningly admonishing* MOTHER MARGUERITE.

ROXANE: [*whispered*] You haven't flirted with the Sisters.
CYRANO: Ah yes, of course ... I just hope Sister Martha is not wearing white today, she's too pale for white, she just can't carry it off; and Claire's hat last week was dreadful, she looked like a confused pelican ... Oh, I'm sorry, were you listening?
MOTHER MARGUERITE: Monsieur de Bergerac.
CYRANO: [*standing with difficulty*] *Mea culpa.* A quick confession. Sister Martha, show me those eyes. Ready?
[*And with deep solemnity*] I ate meat yesterday. I ate a thylacine. They're an endangered species. I felt terrible afterwards, though.

> *Beat.*

So I ate a bison.

> *A small collapse.*

SISTER MARTHA: Monsieur, you must come to the refectory after, for a bowl of soup, you are so pale. Please? Just once.
CYRANO: No, I'm full! Where is Pelican Head? Ah, you'll need to sit to hear this—I ate a Good Samaritan.
SISTER CLAIRE: Monsieur Cyrano!

ACT FIVE

CYRANO: He wasn't looking, never knew what bit him.
But here's my real surprise, ladies.

The bell for vespers rings.

MOTHER MARGUERITE: Come to prayers, Sisters.

CYRANO: Tonight I give you permission ... This will surprise you!
Tonight, you can pray for my soul.

ROXANE: There's a breakthrough.

SISTER MARTHA: I've been praying for you already, monsieur. *Au revoir.*

The NUNS *exit.* CYRANO *gazes at the scarf, disappearing well into the distance.*

CYRANO: How is that scarf going? Any progress?

ROXANE: I can't bring myself to stop ... it's my lifeline. As is my *Gazette*!
Are you ready to report.

CYRANO: Of course.

ROXANE: You seem melancholy today.

CYRANO: Not at all, just that bison is repeating on me.
Right.
Saturday last ... the nineteenth—The President was struck down with a bout of democracy, he became temporarily competent ... but parliament gave him an enema, and normal service was resumed.

ROXANE: Cyrano, taste levels please.

CYRANO: Sunday—next day—ah, yes. Versailles hosted a ball, they filled the Great Hall with seventeen thousand, six hundred and sixty-three white candles—but somebody wet the matches.
Monday—A bishop went to heaven! Yes, they've declared it a miracle.
Tuesday—Nothing. But the candle scandal brought its first casualties, three treasury officials lost their wicks.

ROXANE: Cyrano ...

CYRANO: Wednesday followed, as usual. Lady Lydia took a new lover.

ROXANE: Ohh ...

CYRANO: And that afternoon, Lady Lydia took a *new* lover. At five o'clock, Madame Argent said no to Monsieur Brousie.
Thursday—twenty-fourth—Nothing very important, Europe slipped closer to another war, but no-one was too troubled. A little German man has grown a tiny moustache to draw attention from his nose, I wish I'd have thought of that.

Friday—Montfleury died.
He was disembowelled and France rose three feet above sea level.
Oh, and Madame Argent said yes ... but Monsieur Brousie wasn't listening.
And Saturday—today ... the twenty-sixth ...

His eyes close. Is he gone? ROXANE *turns amid the silence.*

ROXANE: Cyrano. Are you tired? Cyrano.

He stirs.

Did you faint?

CYRANO: What? What is it? No, no, I was ... It's nothing.

ROXANE: You're not well.

CYRANO: No, it's the old wound ... from Arras ... it, ah, sometimes ... you know ...

ROXANE: [*sitting beside him*] Dear old friend.

CYRANO: It's nothing. There, it's gone.

ROXANE: We both have old wounds. Mine still aches, here. The paper crumbles, it still bleeds and weeps. His blood and tears.

CYRANO: May I read it? You once said I could.

ROXANE: His last letter? ... You never wanted to.

CYRANO: Today ... I would like to.

He takes the wrapped handkerchief from her breast.

May I?

ROXANE: Open it. Read it.

CYRANO: [*reading*] 'Goodbye, my Madeleine, today I shall die ...'

ROXANE: Aloud?

CYRANO: [*reading*] 'Death comes at last to all men. But true love, to so few.

Your pardon, Roxane, my words feel heavy today.
They carry a weight too great to bear—
Our future, never to be revealed;
Our eyes, never to meet again;
Our mouths, never to find the words,
Upon which our hearts depend.'

ROXANE: Have you read this letter ... before ...?

CYRANO: [*reading*] 'So if words are no longer our friends, I give you my tears.

ACT FIVE

> I bequeath them you, Roxane, see your reflection in them, my love.
> I cannot write. So I cry.
> And my tears make one word. Goodbye.'

ROXANE: The way you read ... your voice ...
CYRANO: [*reading*] 'Take these scratches of my pen, and hear my voice in them;
> Take this paper that I fold, and know my choice again ...
> Always and ever, is you.'

ROXANE: You can't have read this before ...
CYRANO: [*reading*] 'I love you, Roxane. I love you.'
ROXANE: Your voice ... that voice ...
CYRANO: [*reading*] 'I see you now, in my favourite gesture, the way you brush that strand of gold from your face. Never for one second has my heart been absent from its place, in your hands. Goodbye, my angel.'

> ROXANE *turns to look at him.*

ROXANE: [*with certainty now, reciting, not reading*] I know that voice.
CYRANO: [*reading*] 'I forever remain the one,
> In this world and the next,
> Beyond the dying of the sun,
> The moon and tides at rest,
> Beyond the time of dreams, and ghosts,
> Beyond what's evergreen,
> The one who'll love you best and most,
> The only love there's been ...'

ROXANE: The light has gone. How can you read?
CYRANO: What?
ROXANE: It's dark.
> *Silence.*

For fourteen years on end, you have come here as my friend, to amuse me, to sit, to talk, and you never said a word—
CYRANO: Roxane.
ROXANE: It was you.
CYRANO: No, Roxane, no.
ROXANE: I should have heard it, every time you spoke my name, every time you took my hand ...
CYRANO: No, Roxane.

ROXANE: There it is again ... Roxane ...
CYRANO: It wasn't me.
ROXANE: It was you.
CYRANO: No.
ROXANE: The letters ... were yours.
CYRANO: No, his.
ROXANE: That voice in the dark ... was yours.
CYRANO: I swear it was not.
ROXANE: It was your soul. That mad, impossible soul.
CYRANO: I did not love you.
ROXANE: You did. You do.
CYRANO: He did.
ROXANE: You do. You're already giving in.
CYRANO: No, no, my one love ... I don't love ...
ROXANE: For fourteen years, these silent tears ... were yours ...
CYRANO: [*giving in*] But the blood. The blood is his ...
ROXANE: Such silence. Why today? Why today?
CYRANO: Because—

    LE BRET *and* RAGUENEAU *enter.*

RAGUENEAU: [*calling*] Cyrano!
LE BRET: He's here.
CYRANO: Of course he's here.
LE BRET: You should know, madame, he's killed himself to come to you.
ROXANE: Oh God, that faintness ... his exhaustion ...
CYRANO: Yes, I regret,
    I rudely interrupted my *Gazette*,
    On Saturday, twenty-sixth, an hour before dinner,
    Bergerac was foully, stupidly, murdered ...

    He has removed his hat.

RAGUENEAU: He was ambushed in a lane.
ROXANE: What? What are you saying? What happened?
CYRANO: Destiny mocks me, as ever ... I promised myself a soldier's end, with a piercing epigram on my lips, a real cracker ... but an inglorious life deserves an ignoble death ... killed by a lackey, too scared to face me, who drops a lump of wood from a window. Through every act of life, I missed my cue, and at the curtain, I missed my death too.

ACT FIVE

RAGUENEAU: No, Cyrano.
CYRANO: No tears, tell me, my friend. Are you writing?
RAGUENEAU: I work for Camus ...
CYRANO: [*with proud relief*] Ah! Albert.
RAGUENEAU: I do his laundry.
CYRANO: Ah.
RAGUENEAU: But I'm quitting, it's too painful. Yesterday I saw his latest, he has stolen a whole scene from you?
CYRANO: What scene?
RAGUENEAU: The hotel room, right down to the line: 'Autumn is another spring, when every leaf's a flower'.
LE BRET: He stole that?
CYRANO: What's it matter? It's a good one to steal, and I wasn't using it. But did the scene work, Ragueneau?
RAGUENEAU: It worked. They laughed, and laughed.
CYRANO: The story of my life. Prompting others. From the wings. In the dark.

The bells.

They're coming from prayer now. Nymph, in thy orisons, etc ...
ROXANE: Sister. Mother Marguerite.
CYRANO: [*entering delirium*] Do they bring music?
ROXANE: You mustn't go. Cyrano. I love you.
CYRANO: Don't say that, my princess. This toad will never change.
ROXANE: I can't forgive myself. I've made you so unhappy.
CYRANO: [*suddenly, refreshingly lucid, momentarily*] No. God. Are you kidding? You are my only happiness. [*An emphatic announcement to all*] I have a confession. I've had little experience with women, and less with affection ... Words were my game, never girls. My mother found it hard to look at me. My sister ... could *only* stare. I was never called son, or brother. Except by you. I knew a woman could never love me, but you gave me friendship. Without you, I would not, I could not, have known the joy, the inestimable privilege of a woman's company.
LE BRET: [*seeing the moon*] Your other friend has come too. To see you off.
RAGUENEAU: A blue moon.

ROXANE: I have loved but one man in my life.
And now I lose him twice.
CYRANO: Tonight, I test my theories of flight.
LE BRET: It's not fair, it's unjust. To die like this. So great a heart.
CYRANO: There he goes again, my moaning friend, Le Bret.
'We are the Gascony Cadets, of Captain de Castel Jaloux'—it's really just an elementary mass of—what?—Copernicus would have an opinion on that—
RAGUENEAU: He's delirious. So much learning.
CYRANO: There are more things in heaven and earth, Ragueneau, than are dreamt of in your filos. The rest is ... something, I forget. Here lies Hercule Savinien de Cyrano de Bergerac. Who tried everything, and did nothing. Sinking without a trace. No, no—to the moon.

He tries to stand, but fails.

ROXANE: Hear me, Cyrano. I love you. I love you.
CYRANO: Don't mourn less for Christian. Just add me to the store.
ROXANE: I do. I will. Farewell, my love.
CYRANO: No, not sitting down—no way, José. Here he comes. I can feel it.
Don't help me—Okay, maybe just the tree.

He is standing.

He's coming. I'll wait here. He'll find me on my feet.
My sword—in my hand.
LE BRET: Cyrano, sit down.

RAGUENEAU *gently intercedes with* LE BRET.

CYRANO: Oh. There he is! He's looking at me! He? She! Who knew! What—and looking at my nose! Who are you to mock, Death's Head? [*To the others*] She has no nose. So how does she smell?
RAGUENEAU & LE BRET: [*together, quietly providing him his punchline*] Awful.
CYRANO: Awful! You hear that?! Now, we fight!
But not a fair fight, nothing fair in that.
Better to know the fight is impossibly, irreparably in vain. A hundred to one—
All my old enemies. I see you now ...

ACT FIVE

Hypocrisy.
Falsehood.
Compromises! So many of you!
Prejudice.
Ah, cowardice, always bringing up the rear.
No, not quite, one other hiding there, my dearest enemy: stupidity.
I knew you'd come for me again. *En guard!* I'll fight. To know I'll lose, there's the rub.

> *Again, collapsing, wild despair and ferocity mixed—the final throes:*

You take it all, the laurel and the rose.
You take our joys, our mortal coils, our woes,
But I know the special thing that you've come for,
The one true thing you crave among my store,
It goes with me tonight through that threshold,
It won't be sullied, never bought or sold,
A thing unstained, it outlives death and doom,
You see it, but you'll never have this plume,
It soars above the battle's mud and ash,
It stays with me, one thing …
ROXANE: [*kissing him*] … this!
CYRANO: *My panache!*

> *He dies in* ROXANE*'s arms.*

THE END

Joseph Del Re (left) as Haemon and William Zappa as Creon in Sport For Jove's 2016 production of ANTIGONE. *(Photo: David McCarthy)*

ANTIGONE

A NEW ADAPTATION BY
DAMIEN RYAN
FROM THE ORIGINAL BY
SOPHOCLES

for my beautiful boys,
Oliver and Max:
never lose the child inside

'The time is now and the moment is yours to grasp. Go and get your boots dirty in the field. Go and smell, taste, feel, see, hear and cry with your peers, so many of whom are starving for love, aching for release from the grip of conflict, hoping that one day they will find again their inner world of childhood ... a chance of being safe and happy.'

> Romeo Dallaire, Lt. General, Canadian Armed Forces [Ret'd], a United Nations member dedicated to solving the global catastrophe of the child soldier.

INTRODUCTION

> With august gesture the god shows us how there is need for a whole world of torment in order for the individual to produce the redemptive vision.
> —Friedrich Nietzsche, *The Birth of Tragedy*

The aim of this interpretation of *Antigone* is to offer audiences a contemporary experience of Sophocles' essential theme—the individual conscience struggling against the power of judicial law and the state—while maintaining Sophocles' classical form and sense of poetic justice. That struggle between written and unwritten laws is an eternal and inspirational conflict. But inspirational to whom? The enemy of the state, the 'terrorist', is enacting the same story. Breaking judicial laws, destroying states, committing atrocities for a perceived greater moral or religious good—or indeed, according to the dictates of 'personal conscience'. It is this parallel perhaps, above all, that drew me to Sophocles' play. It asks very challenging, almost objectionable moral questions of any society, both of its government and the individuals it serves.

In writing this adaptation, my focus—and that of my co-director and long-time collaborator, Terry Karabelas, whose contribution to this script, production and to my understanding and appreciation of Greek theatre, has been immeasurable—was on the argument—the 'agon'—above all else. The clash of equal ethical claims over an issue that has not gone away for two millennia and probably never will. Nor has the human cost of warfare. We sought to bring Sophocles' argument alive in a distinctly local and accessible idiom; poetic and straightforward. I have maintained a full chorus and its function, including song and dance. All of the cast operate as the voice of the city, with a strong focus on the female voice, engaging with the political future of their state. The production featured seven women and four men.

Two millennia since it first played in an Athenian amphitheatre, *Antigone* has become an increasingly strange story, with an ugly and macabre synopsis—in burying a criminal's body that her uncle wishes to leave rotting in the sun, a young girl brings herself and her state to its knees. It touches a very modern nerve.

Sophocles captures a burning moral question that has intensified every year since he wrote it. How do we reconcile our hatred and fear of those who seek to hurt us, and how should we punish our enemies? The play is not purely about burying a body: it is about how we bury our own hatred, how we resolve it, salve it, cure it, perhaps even forgive it and reconcile it back to peace. And perhaps the tragedy is that it's impossible. Perhaps? In an interview I made with a soldier about his enemies in the conflict zone, and about the possibilities of forgiveness and honour in death, he said, 'We can all promise to bury the hatchet, but we remember where we buried it'.

When Sophocles wrote this play, there were those in his audience who had seen the advent of democracy in their own lifetime—not just any democracy, but the first the world had ever known. It's an extraordinary thought for those of us lucky enough to have grown up in stable Western democracies today. And yet, for people living in the many failed democracies of the twentieth and twenty-first century—some found through peaceful political evolution, but most through conflict, *coup d'état*, or the intervention of superpowers—the experience of witnessing the birth of a democratic promise is probably as extraordinary as it was for Sophocles' family. This most fragile of political ideals came to Athens only decades before Sophocles' plays first came to the stage. It was a different model to our understanding of democracy, and was of course a purely patriarchal vision of political equality—it was no democracy for the females of the human species. But, notwithstanding, it was a form of 'direct democracy'—*demos*, from the people. We now have a complex representative democracy that is as difficult to define as it is to live in.

Fifth-century Athens and twenty-first-century Australia appear to me to be confronting the same difficulty: how to maintain an effective and practical democracy in the face of infinite compromise and the ever-present threat of corruption? Democracy is a system of governance intended to ensure a community and the individuals within it have some control over their fate or political destiny. *Antigone* deals in the fear that the democratic machinery of power is ceasing to function properly, failing to represent the unwritten laws of conscience that form the basis of an actual individual life and the fabric of a community, toppling us into sometimes subtle and sometimes tangible forms of political oppression. Creon begins to reject the advice of his chorus and the views of his *polis*; leaving his people to feel they aren't 'citizens' of their own state.

Sophocles' audience sat in the open air in 441 BCE to watch a story unfold—one they knew well, a part of the great Oedipus myth—in a city called Thebes. Thebes was not a democratic state at all, but a city under martial law and monarchy. Democracy, however, was the undeniable focus of what the audience witnessed and Sophocles knew it. Democracy was the essential undercurrent—it was not the 'setting' of the story but the very nature and action of the play itself. Dialectic arguments, the voice of the weak challenging the power of the strong, moral debate, social and political concepts of right and wrong, justice and mercy: all were being thrashed out through words. Theatre is the tool of democracy in action. We do not see any of the 'events' of the play. We do not see bodies buried, brothers dying, or sons taking their own lives; we hear the discussion that led to those events or emerged from them. A quasi-legal argument between opposing, irreconcilable forces, in an impromptu and utterly unforgiving courtroom.

In a contemporary setting, we have explored a city returned to an almost-ancient state, bombed into the Stone Age by a horrific conflict. There is no power, no hot water, no electricity, no social services. Sophocles was a general and a war poet. He wrote a story in which a city of people awake from the horror of an utterly devastating civil conflict, to celebrate something as simple as seeing the rays of the sun and feeling it on their faces. The only way they can resolve a heated moral dilemma is for the king to come down in person to the public square and talk to his people, without the help of a microphone, asking to be heard, relying purely on words to restore order to the chaos. And in the heat of that public square, over 24 hours of one day, we see a community come to terms with the laws of the living and the dead. Within that world, a chief desire in the writing was to spend time with the women in this story.

While this is essentially a new play, the only real significant shift in dramaturgy is to remove the notion of the two dead brothers (Polynikes and Eteocles) being kings fighting over their right to the Theban throne.

In our story, Polynikes is a young man who has joined the enemy, become entangled with a violent, fundamentalist ideology and sought to destroy his own state, rather than a king wanting a throne back. So our story centres on a leader who makes a zero-tolerance law about the burial of his nephew, a 'terrorist', only to find his own niece becoming the subject of this new law. An ancient public argument, played out on a destroyed modern street. It is a story as much about growing up, and about the seeds of human violence, as it is about violence itself. In Australia, as in any other country, the community must understand its role in the increasing disillusionment and vengeance of young men. The United Nations has recently declared that the child soldier is the most dangerous modern instrument of war. How are we failing our children? And can we see any responsibility at our own feet?

In a review of two other modern reworkings of *Antigone*, Australian theatre-maker and commentator Alison Croggon drew comparisons between the ancient play and current conflicts:

> Last month, a grim drama played out on the Habur border between Turkey and Iraqi Kurdistan. Amid simmering tensions between Ankara and the Kurdistan Worker's Party, a truck carrying the bodies of 13 Kurdish men and women killed fighting Islamic State was refused permission to cross into Turkey, where grieving relatives were waiting to bury their dead.
>
> In searing 50 degree heat, distraught families protested against the government for 10 days, until finally the government relented and let the truck through. 'I want my son to have a grave,' said Abdurrahman Pusat, the father of one of the fighters. 'He is a citizen of Turkey and not any other country.'
>
> The passions unleashed on that border are a contemporary enactment of the conflicts of Sophocles' tragedy, *Antigone*. Here, written in new blood, is the profound need to mourn the dead, pitted against the stark authority of the state; the questions of what it means to be a citizen, and what it means when citizenship can be revoked, even in death. The Turkish opposition leader might have been quoting Antigone herself

when he said, 'People have the right to demand respect for their dead, no matter how they have died'.

ABC Arts, 1 September 2015

An incitement to develop a new production of *Antigone* struck me while listening to a National Public Radio broadcast a couple of years ago. Journalist Deborah Becker reported that:

> A funeral director in Massachusetts cannot find a burial plot in American soil for the slain perpetrator of the Boston Marathon bombing, no cemetery has agreed to accept it. The body lies rotting in the nondescript Graham, Putnam and Mahoney Funeral Parlor in Worcester, Massachusetts. Protesters are gathered outside, angry that the parlour has taken in the body. The Government has refused to step in. Peter Stefan says ultimately his funeral home is responsible for the body, so he wants to make sure it is buried.
>
> 'I want to know for a fact that once I get him there, that someone's going to do something and bury him, not go back and forth and hold the body there because he's a terrorist or whatever they want to call him. I don't know that if I'm not there. I'm not just going to send the body out. I don't care who it is. This isn't what we do.'

'Cemeteries Refuse To Take Body Of Boston Bombing Suspect',
All Things Considered,
NPR, Deborah Becker, 6 May 2013

This report is remarkable. It's a direct demonstration of how the public might come to agree with a leader like Creon refusing to put the 'hated dead' in the ground. When the body was eventually buried in the earth, it was dug up by the furious community and had to be secretly reburied elsewhere.

Sophocles' play points to the pathetic fragility of human institutions and the unknowable nature of what we call God(s) or morality. It reminds us that there are higher principles at work than are reflected in our constructs of human justice or 'written law'. In *Antigone*, the gods embody destiny and dispense justice according to their own capricious code.

In the theatre, it seems to me the challenge lies in our willingness to recognise that conflicting ideas and terrible events form part of a pattern, reflecting the workings of the unknowable, irrational nature of human affairs. While it is hard for us to know what is 'right', we can learn that communication and free discussion are the only roads towards understanding why we suffer so terribly in the act of living. The gods in this play do not act 'justly' in a human sense, but nor do they act arbitrarily or unintelligibly. Their perfect knowledge is set against the inevitably limited knowledge of mortals, who may bring disaster on themselves while acting with the best of motives. Indefinable ideas of justice and human morality play out in front of us in *Antigone*. The play asks us to decide where we believe we stand.

Tragedy's intention is to remind us we are alive. The creative act is by definition a political act when the convention is tragedy. It is a communal act, where the Chorus is perhaps the central character, seeking to renew our respect for life, for the obligations of living; the personal, social, cultural, political, spiritual duties of 'living well'. Being true to ourselves but never simply *for* ourselves. Regardless of what religious model it reflects, it is serving a fundamental instinct for the awareness of something greater than ourselves, something uncontrollable, incomprehensible and absolute. Our 'god impulse'—our internal conflict between *theos* and *polis*. Tragedy asks us: What are our duties as human beings, as opposed to our duties as citizens?

Each generation curates a new way to see the world: new filters, especially for the most intractable and difficult ideas about living. It's interesting the way a play like *Antigone* has changed over the millennia. By the twentieth century, most staged depictions of Creon made him almost automatically the villain and Antigone herself had become a Joan of Arc figure: the righteous underdog, the conscience-driven heroine who refuses to submit to the new law. Antigone has steadily become a tragic victim—a powerful feminist totem fighting against oppression, a great revolutionary fervour crushed—rather than an excessive fundamentalist whose pride and ferocity would have disturbed Sophocles' audience in 441 BCE. The play of course, by its end, does ask us to acknowledge Antigone as more 'right' than Creon, so perhaps that's inevitable.

INTRODUCTION

The moral altercation at the heart of this play is: What do we do with the bodies of those we hate? When played out on a human level every day somewhere on earth, this is terribly difficult to resolve. What do the families of the people who were killed or injured in the Boston Marathon bombing make of young Antigone's heroism? *Antigone* continues to be a subversive and powerful play, inspiration for generations of rebels and dissidents, because its meaning can be inspiring or disturbing, depending on which gods and which interpretation of religious law you choose to exemplify through action.

Warfare is asymmetrical today. No longer armies lined up across plains awaiting a call to charge, it is a horrifyingly unpredictable reality for every person on earth. Death and catastrophe can come from within our own communities, at the most inconspicuous moment, into our cafes, public spaces, homes, transport systems, even in a time of peace. The political voice today is obsessed with symbolic speech and action in response to the random fear that governs us. I stood with my children at a public event in Sydney recently and found myself gazing into the large crowd and thinking what an easy target we all were in that moment. Where would I run with my children if something happened—if a tragedy took place?

Tragedy on stage is a highly organised reminder of our self-limitation. There is just so much we don't know. How do we decide what we believe in and how many of us have the courage to live by it?

Damien Ryan
May 2017

Christopher Tomkinson, Elijah Williams and Thomas Royce-Hampton and Sport For Jove's 2016 production of ANTIGONE.
(Photo: David McCarthy)

Antigone was first produced by Sport for Jove at the Reginald Theatre, Seymour Centre, Sydney, on 6 October 2016, with the following cast:

HAEMON	Joseph Del Re
ANTIGONE	Andrea Demetriades
EURYDICE	Deborah Galanos
BOY (YOUNG)	Marie Kamara
ISMENE	Louisa Mignone
CHORUS LEADER	Fiona Press
SOLDIER	Thomas Royce-Hampton
TIRESIAS	Anna Volska
SENTRY	Janine Watson
BOY (OLDER)	Elijah Williams
CREON	William Zappa

Other CHORUS roles were shared by the ensemble.

Directors, Damien Ryan and Terry Karabelas
Set and Costume Designer, Melanie Liertz
Scenic Artist, Rosalind McKelvey Bunting
Lighting Designer, Matt Cox
Sound Designer (Live Percussion), Thomas Royce-Hampton
Sound Designer and Operator, Bryce Halliday
Fight Choreographer, Scott Witt
Stage Manager and Chorister, Christopher Tomkinson

CHARACTERS

CHORUS, the people of Thebes
CREON, King of Thebes
ANTIGONE, niece to Creon, daughter of Oedipus
ISMENE, her sister
EURYDICE, wife to Creon
HAEMON, son to Creon and Eurydice
TIRESIAS, a blind seer
SENTRY
SOLDIER
BOY [YOUNG], a deaf boy
BOY [OLDER], the same boy, ten years older

The CHORUS, SENTRY and SOLDIER remain onstage for most of the play. If stage entries and exits are not indicated, this should be decided at the director's discretion.

SETTING

The action takes place in a vivid empty space, characterised as a destroyed modern city, but offering easy spacial versatility. The Prologue between the two sisters, one cleansed, the other filthy from the desert plain outside the city walls, takes place in a palace bathroom. The ensuing Episodes One to Three and the Choral odes are placed in a central city square or agora of Thebes. Antigone's Lament takes us inside the palace in her father's abandoned reception rooms. In Episode Four, Creon meets Tiresias in an old town hall set up by Haemon for a public meeting. The final stretch of the tragedy returns us to the palace exterior.

/ in the text denotes an interruption or overlap.

ACT ONE

PROLOGUE

A contemporary world. A decimated city.

A bathtub. Midnight. Stillness. Two sisters. Both exhausted. Heavy pressure in the room. Things are happening slowly here.

ISMENE *sleeps in the bathtub.* ANTIGONE *is watching her. Silence. She wakes her sister.*

ANTIGONE: [*whispering*] Xipna. Xipna.
  [*Violently*] Xipna!
> ISMENE *is startled. Lies back again.*

Kimithikes?
I can't either.
You look good though ... for no sleep.
You looked like you were dreaming. Going into a dream ... coming out of a dream. What were you dreaming about?
> *Nothing from* ISMENE.

The silent treatment.
> *Silence.* ISMENE *starts washing—rubbing oil on her skin.*

The silent ointment!
It's a lacquer, your silence, isn't it? My quiet ... polished sister.
> *Silence.*

It's so hot.
> ANTIGONE *touches* ISMENE*'s back.* ISMENE *flinches sharply.*

I know, they're cold, aren't they? Do you know why they're cold? Do you know why my hands are so cold?
ISMENE: They're always cold.
ANTIGONE: Not like this.
> *Silence.*

It'll happen faster in this heat, won't it? His skin.

ANTIGONE *draws gently on her sister's back with her fingers, begins examining it closely.*

Not yours. You'll turn into a lamp when you die … all light and heat and oil, you'll never decay. You'll liquefy. Bodies are porous, aren't they? They ooze. Like borders, nothing stays in, nothing's kept out, in the end. We should bottle you before you burn away, all that scented sweat. Oil of Grace, we'll call it. Eau de Demure. Eau de-mure. Eau de Manure!

The trivial provocations have no effect on ISMENE.

Always so calm! How do you do it? It's like you've *stopped*. You make things *stop* … don't you, you make boys stop in the street. In the market. Stop and smell the ointment.

ISMENE: Is that our father's coat?
Take it off. Take it off!
ANTIGONE: No. Why?
ISMENE: Give it to me.

ANTIGONE *removes the coat.*

ISMENE: [*in a whisper*] Still smells like him. I didn't know you had this. Where did you hide it?
ANTIGONE: I don't know.
ISMENE: You told me to keep nothing. Throw a black stone over your shoulder, you said, and never think of him again. You said we'd never go back there.
ANTIGONE: *Rixe mavri petra*. And did you throw a black stone?

Pause. ANTIGONE *pulls a small bottle out of the pocket of the coat.*

ISMENE: Where did you get that? When did you start …?
ANTIGONE: Questions, questions. Does it matter? Our brothers are dead. Brandy is traditional at this moment, right?

Offers ISMENE *the brandy.*

Don't worry. It's a good one. Metaxa brandy—

ISMENE *takes the drink.*

Ohh-hoo, she's drinking. Do you want a smoke too?
ISMENE: What's wrong with you, Antigone?
ANTIGONE: You won't talk to me.

ACT ONE

ISMENE: Talk about what?

ANTIGONE: You know what—you know what …

> ISMENE *steps sharply into her towel and prepares to leave.* ANTIGONE*'s restlessness getting more active/dangerous.*

I'll talk to myself, maybe you'll eavesdrop. No, I'll pretend there's a crowd—I'll pretend this is the amphitheatre. This is the orchestra—your bathroom!—Now there's a show! There's a civic duty men would turn up to. Thousands of eyes staring at *your bath*. The old plays in the amphitheatre never start like that, do they? It's always a gate, or palace doors, pillars, strong things. No-one wants a play about weak things. [*Announcing as a herald*] Gentlemen of Thebes, we have no pillars but I give you pillows—

ISMENE: Shut up, you'll wake our uncle—

ANTIGONE: No guards, no gates.

> *She holds up a pair of her sister's underwear.*

Ah, now there's a gate. There's a way in, you men of Thebes, Ismene's threshold—

> ISMENE *hits* ANTIGONE *hard, surprising her, and pushes her fiercely to the ground.* ANTIGONE *lies there, unaffected by it.*

ISMENE: Just give Haemon what he wants, Antigone. You won't find sex so fascinating.

ANTIGONE: Bet the ancients never thought we'd see *those* things in the theatre. Maybe one day there'll be no rules at all. Even an ignorant girl taking a bath will be considered interesting.

ISMENE: I'm not stupid, Antigone.

ANTIGONE: I never said stupid.

ISMENE: But it's what you mean.

ANTIGONE: Meant! What I meant! And I said ignorant, not stupid. At least you're clean. Body and mind scoured. I could eat off your mind.

ISMENE: [*engaging fully now*] What is it I'm supposed to know, Antigone? I feel it too, I've suffered as much as you, / why do you have to—?

ANTIGONE: Suffered! / Your idea of suffering is staying in till the water's cold—

ISMENE: You think you know what everyone's feeling, don't you? You sit at dinner tonight, after everything that's happened, we just want to sit together, sit and eat, the first night of peace and quiet, just our family, and you talk, and talk, tell us all the names of the stars!—through the whole dinner … you embarrass yourself … pushing our uncle because he can't tell you how stars are made! Because you read a lot / doesn't mean you love the night any more than we do.

ANTIGONE: I wasn't really talking about stars, you idiot. /
I thought he might realise something before it was too late.

ISMENE: Too late for what?

ANTIGONE: For him.
And I'm talking to the audience—mind your own business. Put your mask on— [*throwing a lotion bottle in the basin*] perfect for a play—your lacquered mask. I won't wear one. Even if they can't see me from the back, it doesn't matter, they're all looking at you anyway.

ISMENE: [*leaving the room*] Go to bed—

ANTIGONE: They *think* they're looking at you—our audience—but they're confused. [*Direct to the audience*] She's not there. [*Back to* ISMENE] They're like one colossal head, aren't they? Look at them. A many-eyed beast. [*Calling loudly to her audience*] You know where she really is?! She's here! [*Picking up the pillow*] Even when she's not.

ISMENE: [*returning*] You'll wake him, Antig—

ANTIGONE: She's here in the pillow—see the dent?

> *She shows her imagined audience, her pain more obvious now.*

Her soft heavy head. Her heap of hair. Look how deep the impression goes, like wax. *This* is my sister. The heavy sleeper.

ISMENE: I hate you, Antigone.

ANTIGONE: My hands are cold because I've been holding our brother's hand. He only has one now.

> *Silence.*

ISMENE: You went out there?

ANTIGONE: I looked for the other but it got dark. In the sand somewhere. I'll find it.

> *They study each other in silence, neither sure who the other is anymore.* ANTIGONE *breaks, immense grief.*

I'm cold.

ACT ONE 159

ISMENE *rushes to place the coat over her sister, lying together on the floor. Silence.* ISMENE *holds her.*

ISMENE: God, it stinks.

She playfully rubs a sleeve of the coat in her sister's face

Smell it!

Fighting it off, laughter. A beat as they settle.

I try to remember Dad's face, his eyes … some parts of him are as clear as knives and forks, but I can't see his face anymore. That young soldier told me today that we deserved it. 'It's the price of your blood,' he said. He said we'd all pay before it was over, our whole rotten family. 'That's the rules—you all have to pay.' It made me freeze inside.

ANTIGONE: Are you ashamed? Daughter of Oedipus.

ISMENE: Aren't you?

Nothing from ANTIGONE.

Where is he? Why will you never tell me? Where is Dad buried?

ANTIGONE: In happiness. There was a strange joy in his sorrow, Ismene—you should have walked with us.

ISMENE: Don't, Antigone—

ANTIGONE: [*lightly, jovially*] No, you should have heard him, on that last day, laughing, choking with it. He'd lost his voice, from screaming and moaning at the sun, and the stars, and telling every passer-by the story of his eyes. By the end he couldn't get through it without laughing, really laughing. There are donkeys and farmers and bent women in fields who've heard it all, from the man himself. The horse's mouth. He sleeps in strange earth now, as he wished, not in the land he loved, not in a cool curtained bed—maybe the sea—I don't know. He walked away and told me not to follow. So I didn't. I sat and watched the sun step across a rock. I'd never sat and watched the light move before, you can see it moving if you take the time, it moves so fast it's hard to believe a day could take so long to end. Or a month, a year. When you watch the light move it doesn't take very long at all. The sun doesn't wait for anyone.

ISMENE: [*making her point*] So no-one buried him. No-one buried our father, Antigone.

ANTIGONE: [*sharply*] You don't know that.
ISMENE: Neither do you.
ANTIGONE: Athens buried him, or a farmer or an army, I don't know, but he is under the earth. Everything buried him. I did follow him eventually, I looked for him, he's gone. Below. In the land—inviolate, immutable—are they words you understand, Ismene?

> *Beat.*

Help me bury our brother.
ISMENE: We can't, Antigone.
ANTIGONE: The Argyve army is gone, the soldiers left last night. We can do it now. In the dark.

> *Silence.*

> ANTIGONE *tries to lift* ISMENE *off the ground—the struggle is immense,* ISMENE *is a dead weight. Giving up,* ANTIGONE *makes to go.*

I'll do it myself.
ISMENE: Stop, listen to me. Did you hear anything at dinner, / did you—?
ANTIGONE: Of course, / of course I heard, do you—?
ISMENE: Well, you just kept talking so I thought maybe—he's going to proclaim it this morning. Polynikes hated us, Antigone. He killed our brother.
ANTIGONE: He is our brother. Eteocles killed him, he killed Eteocles. They died together, they should lie in the same earth. But Eteocles is to be buried in state, as a hero, as he should—and Polynikes ... out in that heat, his cold fingers, his tiny hands. He was the least of us, Ismene, our little brother.
ISMENE: And I loved him. I raised him, Antigone, more than you ever did. Both of them. But he didn't love me, he forgot you, he left us behind when he joined that army, those killers. He shed blood, Antigone. That poor woman, Aspasia, from the library, / her head, her blood—
ANTIGONE: We don't know, / we don't know that was him—
ISMENE: In the video, it's him, you know it's him, Tig—
ANTIGONE: That's rumour—
ISMENE: The shooting in the marketplace.

> *Silence.*

ACT ONE

So many dead—
That was our brother, Antigone. He chose his path, not Creon. It's not the same at all. We should shut up, not say a word, everyone hates us, the whole city, we should be quiet. Rest and forget and work and … just forget. We've been through enough, haven't we? I don't want to leave him out there … on the ground, alone, I want to hold him too, to hold his hand and sing to him … I don't hate him. But you heard our uncle, anyone who touches his body dies. The people will agree. It's not an idle threat, Tig.

ANTIGONE: [*very simply*] Will you do this with me? Say the words, pour the wine, brandy if you want. Will you help me?

ISMENE: I know the dead will forgive me if I do what the law tells me to.

ANTIGONE *is empty.*

God, you frighten me—

ANTIGONE: No I don't. You do that for yourself. [*Viciously*] The law! You are—

Kicking ISMENE*'s scents and cream bottles over:*

Here, you moisturise, I'll bury our brother.

ISMENE: I'll keep it secret, I promise. I won't say a word.

ISMENE *tries to physically calm* ANTIGONE*'s fevered response.*

ANTIGONE: Yes-you-will-you-better-I'll-hate-you-more-if-you-don't-publish-it-tell-the-world-set-the-gods-on-fire-I'm-not-keeping-secrets-there's-nothing-to-hide-I'll-lie-with-him-happily.

ISMENE: The earth is parched, Antigone—

ANTIGONE: You please the living, I'll love the dead—

ISMENE: You're not even strong enough to break the ground.

ANTIGONE: [*taking up the old urn from beside the bath*] I'll take dirt. I'll be convicted of reverence—

ISMENE: Reverence—

ANTIGONE: You, and Creon, you're the ones breaking a law—

ISMENE: Polynikes would forgive us both, Antigone.

She catches ANTIGONE*, who is leaving.*

Throw a black stone, sister.

ANTIGONE: I will. When it's done.

ISMENE: [*desperate*] It's almost dawn, they'll see you.
You'll fail at this, sister.

ANTIGONE: When I have tried and failed, then I'll have failed.
Stay asleep, Ismene.

> ANTIGONE *moves into the darkness, heaving the urn with her.*
>
> *Deafening sound swells and shunts us into the centre of the shattered city, the people emerging from rubble, wearing dust masks, hard at work seeking survivors, clearing rubble.*

PARADOS

> *Dawn begins to rise—one, then another, then another see it coming. The* CHORUS *speak together or separately as required.*

CHORUS: *Aktida tou Iliou.*
The sun.
Illios!
Welcome!
It's a whisper yet.
But the east can never keep a secret.
Aktida tou Iliou.
The brightest of all that ever dawned
On the city of seven gates, city of Thebes.
Aktida tou Iliou.
The dawn will always choose the mountains first,
It likes to wake with dancing.
On the plains,
The fields,
The long flat roads,
The sun is forced to walk,
Like any mortal.
But in the mountains it can vault and leap
And tumble shadow-first,
Down chasms,
Over caps and crags,
And slide from brink to brae—
Aktida. Aktida tou Iliou.
If we didn't know better,
We'd take that dance for panic.

ACT ONE

Panic that this world that didn't want another day.
Or that Bacchus ruled the sun.
YOUNG CHORISTER: [*calling*] It's in the water! The sun, it's in the river!
CHORUS: The light loves water best,
   No panic there,
   It can improvise
   And let off steam.
   Pano apo ta nera tis Dirkes, irthes.
   Once it ambles down to Dirce's breast,
   And lays its long blade upon the river,
   It gets to rest, and reflect,
   Splash and spray,
   And quench its thirst for movement without even trying,
   Light floats, you see.
   Brings the future to our gates. A golden promise.
   Peace.
   It hasn't always been this way.
   Seven years of darkness
   Crossed Dirce's stream,
   Climbed her bank,
   Scaled our walls,
   Choked our breath,
   Stole our blood.
   We stood in fire.
   In a circle of death,
   With complaining voices, 'The dawn will never come,' we said,
   To lift the smouldering haze.
   We were breathing in our own sadness.
   Ruins ourselves, wandering among ruins.
   A yawning ring of mouths,
   Gasping at pollution—
   But in the day just gone,
   The one that felt like many,
   We rose like a dragon,
   And with our wasted breath
   We shouted *death* in the hated face of Argos.
   Captains fell at every gate—

Theirs and ours,
Friends and enemies,
Like men of snow.
And the storm broke.
With the dusk, last night,
The darkness fled on wings of fire and fear.
Aktida. Aktida tou Iliou.
Then silence.
Isihia.
Telos. O polemos. Telos.
The end.

> *Two* CHORISTERS *dance—wild, combative. Percussive speech and dance collaborate here.*

Two men, two boys, did not hear the hush.
Brothers of a mother's love,
Now lost to hate and guilt and blame,
They fought on, they fought alone.
They ignored the calls
To *stop*,
To *spare each other*,
To hold a moment and see the end of things.
As brothers must,
They made a vow to see each other home—
To death.
They kept their promise.
With twin hands—indistinguishable—
Twin faces,
Mirrors to a common youth,
They tore each other down.
It is, after all, the fate of glass to break.
And their shudders woke the dawn.
But peace woke with the sun,
See it dance!
That now we dance with it.
Let us shake the ground with joy,
Drink the waters of forgetfulness

And make the silence echo.

They dance and chant in the street—bacchanalian in its joy.

Here he comes. Creon wants us together—the city.

FIRST EPISODE

CREON's *following address is punctuated by powerful reactions and movement from the* CHORUS, *using the ensemble to create a crowd of many thousands, gathered in the morning sun, celebrating the end of conflict. The king stands on a pile of shattered bricks and debris to address his people.*

CREON: Can you hear me?

CHORUS: We hear you!

CREON: Good morning. I did a very unusual thing late last night, a lost ritual, I hope you all did something similar. Around a table, in my home—outside actually—on a clear night, I sat with my family … and we ate a meal. A *rationed* meal, before you point fingers.

The CHORUS *laughs.*

There were no sirens, no incendiaries—for forty minutes not even a phone call. I didn't hear the screams of children playing, early days for that, but I didn't hear the screams of children dying either. Just … silence.

The flares and mortars of the Argyve army, the roar of their engines and artillery, the ruthless hearts they wrapped in vests and sent into our cafes and markets to kill us where we lived, those faces from our children's nightmares have turned in retreat.

He holds up a dossier.

This is the confirmation from Chief of Army. They're gone. It's over.

Applause and wild celebration from the people, which CREON *cuts quickly down.*

At a terrible cost. I can't lie to you, you can see it, we're devastated—our city, our infrastructure, agriculture, industry—the power grid. But we didn't talk about war … at dinner, last night. Instead, we spoke about the stars, well my niece spoke about the stars, at some length, and we listened.

The CHORUS *laughs with him again.*

She bemoaned that so many of our Greek names for the stars are gone, replaced with the names of scientific instruments—there's the final frontier of our empire dispatched.

The CHORUS *is again warmed by his disarming spirit.* CREON *gestures to a particular area of sky.*

One in particular she showed us, a constellation called Arcas, one of Zeus' sons. I woke this morning still thinking about it. An arrogant king wanted to test Zeus to see if he was who he said he was—a god—so he invited him over, to dinner, and served Zeus his own son—to eat—his dismembered body. I struggled with my ration during this bit. The test being: can the father, at the critical moment—before he devours him—recognise his own son? Does he have to actually taste him to know who he is? Unfortunately—you can see where this is going—Zeus dined. When he realised his mistake ...

Silence.

Well, it's lucky he's a god. He collected the parts of his son and made him whole again. Made him a constellation among the stars. Arcas.
A god has eaten our children too—I think this was my niece's message to me—a merciless god, the god of war. We fed them to him if the truth be told, as we always do with the young, the strongest, the bravest.

Very personal to the people around him, perhaps taking each by the hand:

I wish I had the power to make them whole again. Or at least to mark the night forever with their light. I can't. But I can help us learn from the *beauty* of their lives, and their sacrifice.
Our old gods taught us something about beauty, didn't they, something that made sense a millennia or two back. 'That which is beautiful is good.' Greece seemed to accept the definition, our artists conceived from it, our architects proved it in the grace of our buildings. Our mathematicians, philosophers, musicians—well, most of our musicians. That which achieves proportion, balance, measure, is beautiful.

His effortless, almost casual eloquence has become more formal now, building to something, a measured intensity.

ACT ONE

The beauty I speak of this morning lies out on the plain, beyond our seventh gate. It is the body of a man, a boy really. His hip is open to the view, the bone splintered to a mosaic, his left hand missing above the wrist, his face cut clean through, like sugar loaf, and his blood pooled deep on the stone beneath him. His skin is already blackening in the heat, flies breed in his wounds. I gazed upon him through the long dawn. When you watch with patience you can actually see the sun move—the steady march of light revealed each cavity and shattered joint of the boy. And in the glare of day I saw true beauty. True goodness. He was my nephew, Polynikes. And his rotting body is the most beautiful thing I have ever seen.

> *A sudden change in* CREON—*a quickly accelerating severity, an awareness among the* CHORUS *that something deeply felt and personal is unfolding for the state.*

It is in perfect harmony with his *crime*, perfect *proportion*, precise *balance*. He was a traitor, to his state, to his god, and to his family. He brought chaos and death to his own people, to his own brother—for there, in the same light, in the same blood, as once they were in the womb, lay Eteocles, his twin, slaughtered and slaughterer, dead in the same moment. But *his* blackening body was not beautiful. This was the hideous death of a hero. A practical death. He will feel our gentle breath, our tears, be given burial, libation and the full ceremonies of the fallen. Polynikes, his brother, who with this lawless militia, said, and I quote, he would 'Kill until the human soul could recognise no god'—he said this on a video while removing the head of a thirty-one-year-old woman who worked at the city library. I knew this woman. She use to press the returns, the paperbacks, with a warm iron so they looked unread for the next borrower, because, and I'll quote her too: 'A book should be like a child opening its eyes for the first time'. He, as I told his family last night, he is going to help us heal.

Now, I made you two promises in the final months of this conflict—that this day would come—and that when it did, we would sleep the sleep of a free people, and awake to find the age of kings dead. I have inherited a chair in that palace. Today we call it a throne, tomorrow just a chair, like any other. We'll put it in the courtyard, you can sit in it and feed the birds! Because tomorrow I join you as the servant of a new master—Democracy. Interim president of an open, multi-party, representative government—

> *Significant and growing applause, shock, raw emotion from his people.*

Accountability, an end to sectarian violence and repressive censorship, real tolerance, real checks on executive authority, free elections, don't imagine it, see it, an economic development zone, investment, employment—Freedom. I'll say it again. Freedom. But understand, new democracies die like lambs. A reborn Thebes will have to play at miracles with time—we must age years in a day. In this day! With tomorrow's dawn, and the next, and the next, while its most vulnerable, our democracy has to open its young branches to the wind without losing its roots to the inevitable storm—because the sun is up today, but storms will come.

My nephew, Polynikes, lying in that sun on the Aonian Plain, is the carcass of a violent ideology—of fear and fundamentalism—and our carrion birds, Thebes' great eagles, the very symbols of our freedom, are already hard at work, picking apart that ideology. They will devour it, tear its flesh to a thousand fragments, carry it high on the winds, and deposit it where it may never again reassemble itself. His flesh gone, his bones will lie on that hot earth, untouched, unburied, unmourned and forgotten. Except by the dogs whose teeth perfect his beauty.

Your king for a day, this is my decree.

Bury him in our soil, anyone, we will unbury him and you will lie with him. Mourn him and you will join him.

Good morning, Thebes. It is a good morning. The sun is up. Let us work.

> *Silence.*

> CREON *steps down from the rubble to move away, but senses the uneasiness among his people.*

You're the voice of this city, you're free to speak.

> *Beat.*

Don't pity my family or my decision. My family is yours, each family is the state's.

ACT ONE

CHORUS: Your family is your own. And each man's family is a mysterious country.
For those who are dead, and for we who remain, for the friend and the enemy, we accept your guidance and your decree.

> *A voice in the distance bellows, followed variously by others in a rapturous echoing cry around the city: 'Mourn him and you will join him!'*

CREON: See then that it be kept. There is already a watch upon the body.
CHORUS: Is that a resource we can afford, sir? Every hand should be at reconstruction.
CREON: Any city can rebuild—this boy's body, festering back to earth, is our moral soil, on it we rebuild our character.

> *A jolt and darkness. Sound pulses to a new moment, sudden and sharp.*
>
> *A* SENTRY *has appeared on the pile of debris. Panting heavily. She is out of breath.*

SENTRY: I'm not out of breath. I mean I am out of breath. But not from running. I wasn't running.
CREON: I don't care if you were. What do you want, soldier?
SENTRY: Sorry, I should have been running I mean. I really should have been. I wasn't. But I'm still out of breath! What a waste! They sent me because I'm the quickest. I've never moved so slowly, I pretty much loitered. I caught most of what you said, sir. Good speech. Not good for me, but generally, good to listen to. So why hurry, I thought. But if you hear it from someone else, that's probably worse, I was thinking, just behind the wall there. Seeing it's my job ... to tell you.
CREON: You're part of the watch. Tell me what?
SENTRY: Just need to catch my breath—
CHORUS: Speak.
SENTRY: Just to be selfish, for a minute—
CHORUS: Speak.
SENTRY: I didn't do it, my lord. None of the watch did. You can't punish us. You can, of course ... probably will—
CREON: Punish what?
SENTRY: It can wait till later, things seem tense now.
CHORUS: What's your name, soldier?

SENTRY: Someone buried the body, sir. The corpse. The nephew-corpse. Not the good one, the bad one—the other one. The terrorist.
CREON: [*sharply*] We haven't used that word throughout this conflict and we won't start now.
SENTRY: Sorry, sir, it seemed to fit the bill—
CREON: There is no terror if we are not afraid. Who did it?
SENTRY: Don't know, sir. There was no sign of a pick or a shovel. The earth is parched, it's quite an effort. We never heard a sound. It happened just after dawn, after you left, sir. The earth is so hard and dry, don't know how they did it. No clues.

And when I said buried, just dust, just covered from sight, not a proper grave, just a layer, like a passer-by maybe … or … maybe a holy burial … maybe … or a dog … probably not a dog—
CREON: You weren't watching?
SENTRY: We were. And arguing. Watching and arguing—over that word, *terrori*—and we fought after that, when we saw it, we accused each other, we went back over everything, it came close to blows. But it wasn't us. I'm just a messenger, sir. We agreed I was the quickest. Sorry I'm late.
CHORUS: My lord, I fear—I feared it when she entered—this is work of the gods.
CREON: The gods love a man who burns their temples? Think before you speak.

The rage of years of personal struggle against corruption bubbles over for CREON.

No, no this is money talking, the wealthy bribing their instruments to do this thing. There's a party in this city—every city but this one is diseased with it—impatient of any power not vested in them. A rotting corpse is bad for business, isn't it! Money is the death of principle. It can devastate as thoroughly as war because it makes people do what their values would reject.

You think me cruel? Barbaric—to do this—my own family? This law? Anyone here think me cruel? Should Thebes be ashamed to face the world because we punish our murderers? I'll say it again. No man's family is above the state. We love our own most when we love our city. [*Referencing elements of the* CHORUS] Our reborn Thebes must reject corruption and silence the power of money to talk.

[*To the* SENTRY] You. What's your name?
SENTRY: Sentry. I mean, sorry?—job or name? Pia, sir, Pia Sanopoulis.
CREON: Were you paid to look the other way while they buried him?

He grabs her hands and studies them.

You do it yourself?
SENTRY: No, sir!
CREON: Find the man who buried that body and bring him to me or you will rot with him. Do you understand me? You will bake on that earth beside him.

The SENTRY *makes to leave quickly.*

But first—get the dust off his body. Unbury him. Now.
SENTRY: Yes, sir. Will do. Hope I haven't upset you, sir.
[*Upon exiting*] May I offer one opinion, sir.
I can't speak for corruption, and I've only met the wealthy in prison, but I feel there is wisdom in what the old women said.
CREON: You let me think about what the old women said. You think about watching.
SENTRY: That's just it, sir. Sometimes we think too much. My little boy does it. He's twelve. Gets all complicated. I often tell him, wisdom's not all up here—in the belly sometimes. When we're hungry we eat! It was a good speech, sir, lots of thought went into that. But can I tell you what my gut thought? When I saw the body, the dust? I thought … I feared it was the work of the gods too, sir.

Silence.

Or probably a dog …
CREON: Find the man. Bring him to me.

The SENTRY *goes.*

[*To the* CHORUS] You fear the gods? I'd fear the dogs.

CREON *exits.*

FIRST STASIMON—THE ODE TO HUMANITY

CHORUS *members.*

CHORUS LEADER: If a dog … or a lion … had hands—
ALL *stop work, pushing it aside, leaning in together.*

ALL CHORUS: Oh good, I love these. Go on.
CHORUS LEADER: And could with hands depict a sacred work—
ALL CHORUS: If they could draw?
CHORUS LEADER: Hypothetically—
If the beasts could draw a semblance of their gods,
What would they make?

> *Beat.*

ALL CHORUS: Given full artistic license?
CHORUS LEADER: Full artistic license.
ALL CHORUS: What would they make?
What shape takes the god of a bird?
What image makes the lizard of divinity?
CHORISTER THREE: Easy.
Horses would imagine them horses,
The oxen would like them to oxen,
And every beast would draw them as themselves.
ALL CHORUS: For every beast seeks only to belong.
CHORUS LEADER: And to belong to a god, it must belong to us.
ALL CHORUS [*except* CHORISTER FOUR]: The gods of men and women are men and women—
CHORISTER FOUR: [*breaking in suddenly*] And what conclusion do you draw from that?
That we invent our gods, is that your point?
We fashion them from lumps of vanity?
CHORISTER SIX: You don't like hypotheticals, do you …?
CHORISTERS FOUR & FIVE: You ask a valid question, but in reverse.
We didn't draw our God, it's he drew us.
CHORUS LEADER: No, you simplify my point—
CHORISTER FOUR: No—no I don't.
You think that we're just dogs that worship dogs?
CHORISTER TWO: [*getting back to work among the debris*] It's never safe to have this conversation …
CHORUS LEADER: Perhaps—or I could be asking a *question* …!
The thing that sets men and women apart
From beasts and birds of prey—and succulents.
That we ask questions.
CHORISTER THREE: An open mind is the beginning of wonder.

ACT ONE

Silence.

YOUNGEST CHORISTER: Why is our life and death a mystery …?
CHORUS LEADER: Regardless of the truth, of who drew who—
CHORISTER FOUR: Of who drew whom—
CHORUS LEADER: *Of who drew what! Whatever—*
  If gods take on the shapes of women and men—
  [*To* CHORISTER FOUR] —and call this narcissism if it helps—
  It's because we are the wonder of this world …

  Silence.

  A rapid fire, excitable, passionate elocution of human progress.

ALL CHORUS: We are the masters of this ageless earth.
  We mine its arteries and energies;
  Take riches from beneath the underworld;
  We the resourceful! We the tireless!
  We map the stars in search of other earths
  And trick a cunning sun-god for his fuel—
  We farm the wind and ionise the air;
  Take power from the liquid-deep blue surge
  Of seas and rivers. We the original!
  We think fast, speak fast, move fast—we're everywhere.
  The settlements and hamlets, hovelled towns,
  That bred our human village are obscured
  To our pampered metropolitan gaze,
  We rattle past them now on superhighways.
  And already—in a brief millennia—
  The invisible impossible is ours,
  Highways of fibre and ephemera,
  Transparency the size of human hair,
  That let us farm the space between the space,
  And yoke it to the bridle of progress.
  We the significant—the exceptional!
  Ti tha feri to avrio? Avrio.
  What will tomorrow bring?

  They touch the stomach of a heavily pregnant CHORISTER *(played by the same actor who plays* ISMENE*).*

Voiceless tomorrow.
But this—
This age of free imagination
Where tricks have made the giant earth so small—
Comes after *errors*, fatal miscalculations.
For now the inexhaustible earth is tired.
Its oceans over-fished, its soils barren,
Its ice perspires and swells an angry sea.
In the catastrophe of over-population,
Our antibodies fight their own efficacy.
Did we ever think we'd be immune to death?!
The one thing we do together, yet alone,
Is die. Evil or good, or old or young,
And who here can tell what law we owe the dead …?

> *Shunted to darkness again, jolted forward, the* SENTRY *appears again among the debris. She is out of breath.* ANTIGONE *is in her custody.*

SECOND EPISODE

SENTRY: Where's the king? Where is Creon? We found her.
It was a woman, not a man. Not a dog.
CHORUS: [*recognising who it is*] Take her out.
Get her out before he comes.

> CREON *enters.*

CREON: Before who comes?
You. Why aren't you on the watch?

> ANTIGONE *stares at the ground, her face hidden among hair and dirt.*

SENTRY: The job is done, sir. This time I ran.
We found her, this girl, setting order to the grave.
Sorry, getting ahead of myself—so much to tell.
Just so relieved!
Nothing like a good win when you're expecting a towelling.
I went back to work, sir, to that place,
The heat's died down, you'll be pleased to know,

ACT ONE 175

Quite mild there now. We swept away the earth,
As you told us. Exposed the body.
Horrendous task, really. Really unpleasant.
A sodden corpse and naked, raw with death.
We sat up on the hill.
Then we moved to the windward side because …

She expresses the smell.

We stayed so quiet, so focused, my lord.
We spread out, every angle.
I did get weary I admit, after a time,
But I remembered what you said about watching the sun move,
Actually watching the light …
Couldn't quite get it, found that a bit dull,
So I sang the song my son loves,
The one about the window and the spider, and the dragonfly—
I added the dragonfly I think—
Then suddenly I couldn't hear myself singing,
There was a whistling, a screeching—the wind, sir—
You must have heard it, a storm of dust, like a plague,
I didn't mind it actually, I hate the blue sky here.
Every day. Every day. It's not right for a war.
A black storm, an enemy that's plainly visible,
I can see it, I can prepare. Give me that—but
Never seen one like this, stripping the bark from trees,
Whipping stones and sticks across the plain,
Blinding and deafening, you couldn't stand against it,
I had to shut my eyes, sir, I had to, we all did.
Then, as it fell still—
There was a screaming, like an angry bird,
Loud as the wind.
For a moment, I thought perhaps there never was a wind,
Just this screaming …
It was her—the noise—the screeching, it was her,
Seeing that body, exposed, naked—she was crying,
The tears were—stabbing her. I wanted to hold her—
But I just watched, sir. We all did.
The body was actually partially covered again, the legs,

From the storm, the dust, as if the gods themselves had …
But she did the rest. She was wild, sir.
She collected dust—it was everywhere now—
In a fine bronze urn she carried. That seemed to calm her.
Then she did it, sir.
She made offerings, three times to the dead,
She poured the libation; she spread the earth,
Thicker than the first time, she really covered the boy—

CREON: And you let her do this, you watched on.

SENTRY: It was hypnotic, sir,
Like the pictures in the books at the library,
It was hard to look away from the colour and the light—
A strange light, orange and blue after the storm.
And we wanted to be certain.
We knew she couldn't escape, and when we moved on her,
She didn't even try to. She smiled, said hello, asked my name.
I didn't tell her, sir, I kept things very professional.
The angry bird was gone, this was a girl, a joyful girl.
I told her we'd seen her. Seen what she'd done.
She said she knew and hoped we hadn't been hurt in the storm,
Which was thoughtful.
I asked her if she knew the law, the new law, about the boy,
I couldn't even finish the question—she said yes.
She admitted it all. Not frightened. Not even mad.
I was jumpy as hell, I might need some leave, sir.
Anyway, she's here. She's there.

CREON: I see no joy now, no pride. Staring at your feet.
I see shame.
Lift your head.
Look at me [girl] —

> ANTIGONE *lifts her face to him.*

[*To the* SENTRY] Are you mad?
You don't know what you're saying. You saw her?

SENTRY: Was I not speaking clearly? We came straight from the plain.

CREON: [*to* ANTIGONE] Do you—is this true?
Antigone?
You deny this.

ACT ONE

ANTIGONE: I don't deny it. These are my hands.

They are filthy with soil and blood. CREON *takes them in his.*

CREON: [*after a time*] These hands are mine, Antigone. These are my family's hands, how could you do this?

ANTIGONE: *For* my family. For you.
[*Almost under her breath*] *Tha me skotosis theie?*

CREON: Shh, shh. *Ti les tora? Stamata na tremis.*

Speaking quickly, perhaps he holds her trembling body.

You didn't know the law. She couldn't have known. It was decreed this morning, she hadn't heard. Take her home. You! Take her home, find her sister, get her washed, into bed—

ANTIGONE: I don't need to sleep. I'm awake. And I'm clean. I'm cleaner than you are, General.

CREON: Uncle, Antigone.

ANTIGONE: General.

CREON: Antig—take her home.

CHORUS: She knows where she is, sir. She has her father's stubborn spirit.

CREON: She is distressed, her brothers / are dead—

CHORUS: Staring at her feet, my lord, it wasn't shame. She was smiling. The girl called her a bird—she was laughing.

ANTIGONE *laughs again.*

ANTIGONE: I liked that.

CREON: You knew the law—the penalty—you understood it?

ANTIGONE: It was plain enough.

CREON: Then why—?

ANTIGONE: *Yiati then to apodixe o Dias!*
Because your law is not of the gods.
[*Calmly and easily*] You have to lead a people now, uncle. I understand.
You have to make decisions, and show the way,
And be seen to show the way.
So you 'think'. And think again. And deliberate.
Weigh up probabilities. And explain them, justify them.
I heard your speech—
A version of it—from Pia, the girl, the sentry—
She did tell me her name—
While we came here, she told me everything.

You spoke of beauty. She was impressed.
The mind of a civilised man is always impressive.
But it's not justice.
CREON: Don't tell me of justice, Antigone.
You honour the man who killed your brother.
ANTIGONE: Like you honour the man who killed my brother.
CREON: Do you know what honour means, girl? Principle?
Polynikes murdered innocents, you thoughtless child.
ANTIGONE: I don't wish to honour either, I just love them.
They loved me.
CREON: Not enough to spare your city. Your home. He joined the enemy,
He didn't care if you lived or died!

> *Silence.*
>
> *He regains control, takes in the crowd, starting to see there may be no turning back from here.*

Not one person here thinks as you do.
ANTIGONE: Not one person here thinks as you do.
But as a group, they don't think.
They decide you're right, because you sound right.

> *She isolates* CHORUS LEADER, *trying to separate her from the crowd.*

Tell him what you *think*. What *you* really think.

> *The* CHORUS LEADER *looks at a colleague.*

No, not what *he* might say, don't discuss it, don't assess it. Speak.
You.
No government! Just justice. What is justice? To *you*.

> *No answer, she turns to another.*

You then, you have a brother.
CREON: Stop this.
ANTIGONE: Answer me!

> *Silence.*

There's no gag like terror, is there, uncle?

> *She turns back to the* CHORUS LEADER, *playing the room with real confidence now.*

ACT ONE

Then we'll talk about the weather. Safe enough there, huh?
Why was there a storm? The dust from the storm? / Why?—
CREON: I won't hear superstition—
The gods sent my niece a storm!
Your vanity is ridiculous, Antigone.
Your pride. Same curse as your father—
ANTIGONE: [*still pursuing the* CHORUS LEADER] *Answer me!*

Turning to ALL CHORUS, *she now addresses the whole group.*

The first time I buried Polynikes,
I carried the earth there myself, in an urn of our mother's,
I dragged it through the darkness.
My sister told me the ground was parched, that I'd never break it,
So I took the soil from your gardens.
Living soil. Cool from the midnight earth.
Cool on his skin …
The second time, I had nothing,
His body exposed on the burning ground.
[*A rage exploding from her soul*] *Unburied!*
But the storm came when I cried out,
The dust came and I buried him deep.
Tell me why? Why did the wind blow?
CREON: Fetch her sister.

The SENTRY *leaves.*

You are alone here. They pity you. I do.

He is unable to resist the argument.

What is justice?
Justice is community, Antigone, jurisdiction, particular to place and circumstance, an agreed principle that gives men and women trust that every situation may be treated alike, for punishment or reward.
Justice is not the will of a traumatised girl.
ANTIGONE: Nor of a vulnerable man.
CREON: We need order now, you stupid girl, we need law and order.
ANTIGONE: Good. Make laws—for the living.
But who here knows the law of the dead?
CREON: You claim to know. That's precisely what you claim, isn't it?

To know god's law?

The passion of her intellect is at full force now.

ANTIGONE: [*very rapidly*] If you want to call it that.
I know what's unalterable, unassailable.
We all do.
Today you wrote a law, uncle.
Tomorrow another, last week, yesterday …
But a crime for one generation is tolerable for the next.
Isn't it? Permissible even.
We celebrate customs once punishable by death.
Does justice patiently await our enlightenment, does it? Uncle?

Visibly sarcastic now:

What else? Does it acknowledge sovereign borders, airspace …?
Does it pay excise tariffs?
Is justice just geography?
A guilty man in this jurisdiction is proud and free in the next.
That's not justice. That's … management, crowd control.

CREON: Then what is it, Antigone?

Beat.

ANTIGONE: Justice is knowing what to do … when we don't know what to do.

CREON: Conscience. Yes? Conscience?

Beat. ANTIGONE *does not respond.*

Then we agree. And if her conscience differs from yours? Or his? [*Starting to play the crowd as she did*] What then? A *system* of conscience, perhaps? Starting to sound like *government*, isn't it? We set down principles today that we can live by tomorrow—

ANTIGONE: I don't care about tomorrow. About who or where, or what is written.
A man's edict, even a tyrant's, cannot overturn what is unwritten.

She is striving now, the pressure is affecting her.

My brother is not of yesterday and today, but everlasting.

CREON: And there's a girl's manifesto! A government sensible of emotion,
With a deficit of sense.

ANTIGONE: Again. Perfectly phrased!
[*To the* CHORUS] It must be such a pleasure living here. No burden of humility.
CHORUS WOMAN: I see little humility on either side, may I suggest the debate remains civil.
ANTIGONE: [*to her*] Nice to hear from you. At last!
Yes, uncle, please execute me civilly, don't break a sweat.
CREON: There's no debate. Your brother is your enemy, niece.
By his choice.
Your enemy does not become your friend by dying.
ANTIGONE: No dead man is an enemy to anyone, uncle.
He's just dead!
CREON: [*for her alone*] I'm trying to save you, Antigone—
ANTIGONE: You can't.
CREON: What? That's your answer?

He makes to leave.

Get her out, keep her under guard.
ANTIGONE: You said you looked at him. In the sunlight. Did you see him?
His mouth, soft and open … a dead child.
CREON: [*returning*] And what of Eteocles? He's *just dead* too.
Because he did his duty to you.
Died defending you. Me. All of us here.
You insult him, you insult his love. You can't see that, niece?
ANTIGONE: [*coldly*] Eteocles is dead and cannot accuse me of that.
CREON: *You hear this girl?!*
He's dead, yes. And we have a duty to the dead.
Not as you think, not in your actions in that field.
Not to give equal honour to good and bad.
ANTIGONE: Who knows? Do you know that?
CREON: Here's what I know.
[*To a* SOLDIER] You, soldier. Here! Tell her about the girl, the girl from the village—
CHORUS: Elefitheria Agathe.
CREON: Beautiful name, rolls off the tongue, doesn't it, Elefitheria Agathe. Tell her.
SOLDIER: We were sent to protect a village, in the outlying districts, the enemy had been using it to resource but they'd exhausted it and now

they were just pulling it to the ground. We got there too late, the men were dead, the women and girls had had their hands cut off the day before … One of the girls, Elefitheria Agathe, had asked a young man why he was cutting her hands off, why he didn't just kill her—he said, 'We're not going to kill you. We don't want you to vote.' He said, 'My uncle will soon be President—go and show him what we did to you. Show him you won't be able to vote for him.' He told her to 'Ask your president to give you new hands'. Then she said to me, as she went unconscious, 'What is a president?'

Silence.

CREON: We need strength now, clarity, strong symbols, no ambiguity, and if a citizen is not with us, they are against us. Your brother took her hands, Antigone. Do you think she begged him? For mercy? To keep her hands? I think she did. What mercy should I show him? Her hands were his symbol, pretty unambiguous. Now I'm sending ours.
I'm sorry you had to hear that.
But do you understand now who he was?

ANTIGONE: Yes. He was guilty. And I am guilty.
Guilty of holding his love in my conscience.
So today I buried my mother's boy. There is no argument.
That was my *symbol*.

> *The* CHORUS *attacks her, trying to knock her brains out on the bricks—a wild destructive fire in them. They are restrained by the* SENTRY *and* SOLDIER. *The girl is pulled away to the floor, crying out:*

I will not be found guilty of *not* doing that.
Now let me die, and rot, and the sun can judge my beauty.

CREON: It's easy to die, Antigone, it's life takes real courage—

> *The* SENTRY *returns with* ISMENE.

CHORUS: The other girl, the reasonable one, is here.

> CREON *swoops upon her, a fist full of her hair, and drags her away.*

CREON: You viper. You lurk in my house and suck the blood of this family.
You and her. I took you in, the silent agreeable girl.
You humiliate me?

CHORUS: Ribbons of love roll down the poor girl's face.
CREON: [*quickly*] You buried the boy, you share in this. Yes?
ISMENE: I did—yes—if she will let me say so.
  But not to humiliate you, uncle. Or defy the city.
  I love my sister, I am to blame for letting her go.
CREON: Get them out. I'll deal with them shortly.
ANTIGONE: She's lying. She did nothing. She wouldn't share in the work,
  And won't share in the honour. Leave her to shame.
ISMENE: Antigone, don't. I'm not ashamed to stand beside you,
  I want to share your trial, I was proud when you left this morning.
  I believe in my sister, uncle, I believe she is right and you wrong.
ANTIGONE: Who *did it*, Ismene? Who *did it*?
  Who held him in the darkness? Not you. The dead are witness.
  Your love is thought.
ISMENE: Sister—
ANTIGONE: I'll love no sister made of words.
ISMENE: I'll die with you, it's not words, Antigone, we'll go together.

From left: Chorus (Elijah Williams, Fiona Press, Deborah Galanos and Marie Kamara) with Andrea Demetriades as Antigone and Thomas Royce-Hampton as the Soldier in Sport For Jove's 2016 production of ANTIGONE. *(Photo: Marnya Rothe)*

ISMENE *tries to lift her sister from the earth—a dead weight. A desperate* ISMENE *strains at the futile effort, just as* ANTIGONE *did her in the bathroom. Finally,* ANTIGONE *pushes her violently. The* CHORUS *startles at the excessive aggression.*

CHORUS: This is the fever of the mind, my lord. She is mad—
CREON: She was from her birth. The other [*referring to* ISMENE] lately crazed.
ISMENE: Her fever is grief!
Why is a man's grief noble, in women we call it madness?
You condemn her birth, uncle? Her *father* is her *brother*!
What suffering at birth is possible beyond hers? Beyond ours.
Her heart was dead then, what hope but she
Would love the dead more than the living?
ANTIGONE: Don't speak for my heart, Ismene. I love the living,
And not only you.
ISMENE: And I love you, my sister—
[*To* CREON] I won't live without my sister.
CREON: You have no sister. Count her dead already. Take her in. Keep her under house arrest.
ISMENE: It's your son she's talking about—
The one she loves among the living.
You would take her from him? Your own son?

> CREON *learns it for the first time,* ISMENE *is stunned by the realisation.*

You know nothing of them, do you?
Absent father.
My sister was right, she wasn't talking about the stars.
Will you recognise your son before you swallow him whole?
He worships her, she is his first. She will be.
He will never let you take her—
CREON: He'll find someone else.
CHORUS: Sir, speak to him. Meet with him.
The girl is right. Her punishment will be his.
CREON: My family is my country, you said—superannuated fool.
You tell me now what to do with my family?
CHORUS: And each family is the state's, you said, my lord.
We would advise yours as ours.

CREON: Take them in.
  Take them!
CHORUS: Will they die, my lord?
CREON: The one will.
  The other lacks the strength of any conviction
  And can live with what she lacks.

SECOND STASIMON—

A CHORUS *of the three older women, left sitting among the rocks.*

CHORUS: Lucky the one who doesn't see it coming,
  I hope I'll be oblivious on the day.
  This girl,
  Havoc!
  It's her home,
  She's never known another,
  It's her home,
  She was reared in darkness
  From the beginning;
  When she first opened her eyes to the light,
  She couldn't see to see another way.
  It's her home,
  This famous family once the drank the sunlight,
  But mortal arrogance transcends virtue.
  Once heaven shakes a house, it won't let go,
  Or if it does, it's just to shift its grip.
  Each generation hopes the worst is over,
  So we breed on,
  We can't help it.
  Disaster is an aphrodisiac,
  And human nature falls in love with grief.
  Even this girl—
  Love for a boy fills her dead heart.
  Her little pleasure is the spring of sorrow.
  And sorrow craves to breed afresh tomorrow.
  This girl,
  It's her home,
  Hear the song of destruction.

They then sing in Greek as HAEMON *takes the stage. In the glaring midday heat of the square. He is alone. He screams for his father, his voice echoing around a city that has emptied into the shade and shelter.*

HAEMON: *Dad! ... Dad!*

He calls, and waits.

THIRD EPISODE

CHORUS: War was more peaceful than this morning's peace—
Your son is here.

CREON returns to the square, and stares at his son, with no response. Music/sound is swelling to a bursting blister and stops. CREON *holds* HAEMON'*s gaze, a moment of confusion.* CREON *seems unable to engage, unable to recognise his boy—a still, held moment.*

Your son, sir.

CREON: Yes. You look pale, son.

CHORUS: He's been visiting the wounded,
And marshalling the food supply since dawn—

HAEMON: No, nothing so useful. I've just been helping Mum at the hospital.
Good morning, Dad.

Shaking his father's hand, great warmth, he remains holding the hand, looking at it.

CREON: How is she holding up?

HAEMON: She said there'd better be leftovers!

Beat.

Dinner, last night.

CREON: Oh—no, we had it all, I'm sorry. I thought / she'd have something there.

HAEMON: She was joking, just hated missing out. She ate at the hospital.

He has not released his father's hand.

A strange silence, a searching moment.

ACT ONE

I spoke to a man who stopped a bullet with his hand. Really. Said he saw it coming and put his hand up [*gesturing*] —I guess you would— and stopped it. The bone there.

Still holding his father's hand, pressing it, he studies it as he did ANTIGONE*'s. He kisses it.*

CREON: Lucky man.

HAEMON: I said that. He said, 'Not for a drummer!'

They laugh.

There's still no electricity / at the hospital—

CREON: I know—

HAEMON: They're working in the dark—

CREON: We're fixing it. Tomorrow it'll—

HAEMON: They're outside now the sun's up, / generators outside—

CREON: I know, I told her, / by tomorrow, or tonight—

HAEMON: She's operating outside, / they need equipment, drugs, trained staff ...

CREON: Yes, I know, son!

A first sign of exhaustion and defeat in CREON, *one he cannot hide.*

It's chaos, isn't it?

HAEMON: No, it's not actually. People are ridiculously organised, aren't they? They're donating blood, groups of people are standing in lines outside the Supreme Court building, someone put up yellow tape and a guy is shouting, 'O negatives here, we need O negatives,' and two women are writing blood types on people's sleeves, big black letters, everyone is very calm and ordered.

Beat.

But there's no-one there to take the blood. No vehicles, no equipment, there's nothing. Just lines of people with 'O negative' written on their arms.

Beat.

It is very organised, though.

CREON: Sit down. There's a breeze here at least.

HAEMON: Lots of unexpected breezes now, holes in everything—

There is something deeply restless in HAEMON, *unsettled.*

CREON: Haemon—
HAEMON: Maybe you should throw a party, Dad. Not what people expect I know, but surprise them—
CREON: Haemon—
HAEMON: Not winning, just celebrating—
Dionysus came from Thebes, didn't he?
CREON: Yes, he did.
HAEMON: He'd approve. But I suppose you'll say we have to be / practical—
CREON: Practical—yes we have to be practical—
HAEMON: Does anyone have plumbing, I need to go—
CREON: Sit down.

He catches him as HAEMON *attempts to walk past him.*

So much death. [*Holding him*] But I still have my son.
HAEMON: Okay then, practical.
[*Suddenly*] I think we should go district by district and meet the people, Dad.
Town meetings, you know, to talk to the peop—listen to the people … We need to start again, make them feel safe. We could start today, I set up the school hall near the hospital. I put the chairs in sort of circles, you know, made the rows curve so it doesn't feel like—like ranks, you know—when I set them straight, they looked like they were … marching … the chairs—
You know, like they were … If we make the rows curve it feels more …

He can't find a word. Emotion almost overwhelming him, he makes a gesture with his arms, an embrace.

CREON: Haemon, I want to talk to you.
HAEMON: I went up on the balcony, it looked a bit like a violin.
CREON: Haemon.
HAEMON: No, *I* want to talk. I was doing the chairs for this town meeting—
CREON: We're not having a town meeting, Haemon.
HAEMON: A little boy came up to me, a young deaf boy, he signed but he also spoke, with that atonal voice, you know, of someone who's deaf.

There's thirty-five thousand people in this district, Dad, we don't know this kid, we don't know anyone, we have to get to know these people, Dad.
CREON: We will, son. Listen to me—
HAEMON: He looked me right in the eye, this kid,
And said he had killed people.

Brief silence.

His family farm was attacked and his brothers were killed, and his father, and he had to fight, and he killed people.
CREON: They were enemies, son.
HAEMON: But he killed people.
CREON: Enemies. Killers.
HAEMON: People. People. And he was sorry, he said, he was sorry, he didn't mean it. He said he shot anyone who approached the farm, including the old crazy woman who walks the roads, the one who always complained if there were potholes or trees touching the wires. We won't hear from her again. Prob'ly for the best. Potholes everywhere now. I didn't know what to say to him. I just hugged him. He was fourteen. He'd gone deaf in the war four years earlier ... four *years* earlier! When he was ten.
CREON: We'll look after him, Haemon. He'll be forgiv—anyone, everyone—terrible things happened, we'll look after the children, Haemon—
HAEMON: Forgiven?
CREON: The community will accept him back ... forgive him ...

Deep silence.

HAEMON: And when does he get to forgive the community ... how does he forgive us ...? / We stole his childhood—
CREON: We didn't start this ...
I'm sorry for the child, Haemon—
HAEMON: He's not a child, Dad—I don't believe a child can commit a war crime. And I think a girl should be able to bury ...

Silence.

CREON *motions for the remaining* CHORUS *to leave. For the first time, they empty the stage.*

CREON: I'd like to say something, son—

HAEMON: I don't think you should—I don't think you should talk—for a few days, Dad, I think you should listen to the young people.

CREON: [*impatience setting in*] Do you think it's ever been different, has any generation had an idyll for children to live in, Haemon? Do you think it has? A love … and … and … play … utopia? Perpetual springtime.

HAEMON: [*turbulent emotion, as his mind races*] No it hasn't, but they used to grow up at least, they used to teach boys to grow up, the elders chose a time when he got to go into the wilderness and kill off his … boy … self, in safety, in the harbour of grown men who cared for him, of mothers who showed him it's safe to depend on himself now. Today the boy … shoots his boy-self dead in the dark with a console, with no-one watching, and no-one teaching him why or what comes after. And if we try to teach him, he's been *deaf since he was ten*! We need to re-educate, Dad, / a whole generation has learned rape and looting where yours learned calculus.

CREON: I know, son—

HAEMON: Same with the girls I expect—who's teaching them to grow up? I see little girls eyes staring out of women's faces, grown women, little orphans hiding in their heads—no-one gets to grow up here, Dad, / who's raising us, who are our leaders?

CREON: What are you talking about, son, / calm down. I am, I will lead us, I will do better—

HAEMON: Listen to me! Try to follow this, Dad. Antigone's brothers never grew up, Dad, we never let them, they never got to kill the boy inside—to learn to take this—seriously—*that life is serious*—to be men—so they just kept playing the game, like kids, no consequences, never seeing it was a game and now they'll never be men.

> HAEMON *is distraught by this. Silence—hopelessness between them.*

CREON: Well, that's a very evolved thought, Haemon, but—

HAEMON: Evolved? A very—a very evolved thought?! / Would you prefer a less evolved—?

CREON: Haemon, stop it / stop it, stop it!

HAEMON: She just wants them to be touched, Dad, so she knows they're not alone. Both of them. Alike. Will you let her do that?

CREON: So you know. What she did this morning.
HAEMON: She did what everyone is doing, Dad, take a walk! I'll tell what I saw coming here—no, I'll tell you what I didn't see. I didn't see a … form, a complete human form among the dead, there are smudges on bricks, there are halved bodies, families are trying to recognise parts, soldiers are pulling people away from collapsed buildings, but they won't leave because their friends, their families are in there—not even their *bodies*, just viscera, just DNA—they still won't leave them / without holding them, burying them—
CREON: *That's not the same*, Haemon, these are victims, heroes even—Polynikes made this mess, he brought our pillars down, he made the sky fall on us—he made that boy deaf, he took that sense from him, took his innocence. We should honour the *victims*, Haemon, not the devil who did it—
HAEMON: He's not the devil to his sister—
CREON: He doesn't belong to her, she doesn't get to decide, son—
HAEMON: And the dead don't belong to you, Dad—or to her. They're no concern of ours.
CREON: Then who do—?
HAEMON: They belong to the *earth*! And she can see that, that is all.
CREON: And she means more to you than I knew.

   Beat.

HAEMON: That's not why I'm saying / this—
CREON: And you've heard the law?

   A CHORISTER *enters with a small plate of food for them.*

CHORISTER: You should eat.
CREON: Put it there and get out. Thank you.

   The CHORISTER *leaves.*

I can imagine what you think of me. Do you know me, Haemon? No, listen to me, do you think you really know the man your father is?
HAEMON: No, I'm not going to let you spin this, Dad, you'll find a way, / you always do—
CREON: No, we are going to talk, / there's no spin, no-one's spinning, we're talking. You've walked here today with a whole new conception of me, haven't you? I know that, I expected that.

HAEMON: Dad, I need to piss—
CREON: You said men, you said ... *boys* don't grow up. I think you're right. You see things, son, you see through things—you really do. I love that you do that. So I think you can understand what I'm about to say, I think you can. I agree, we've lost our rituals, so many boys, in a no-man's land of ... dry, misdirected energy, aggression, power, sex, big temptations, it's like paralysis. And you're right, you can have parents and still be an orphan—
HAEMON: Not just parents, it's the culture—
CREON: No, I get it—parents, elders, cultural elders, the whole atmosphere we make you breathe—I get it.
   I'm there now, Haemon. Whatever, whoever you think your dad is, is going to be new to both of us from now on.
HAEMON: You're talking again, Dad.

> *Enormous strain in* HAEMON *now, like something stretching inside him that he knows will break.*

What are you talking about ...?
CREON: You can understand this. I know you can. The ancients taught us something, something I only came to understand when I saw the sunrise this morning—
HAEMON: What? *What?!*
CREON: It's impossible to learn anything of a man—his soul, the goodness or poverty of his will, his judgment—until he is seen practising government. Until he leads, and doesn't give in at the fear of leading. Until he is willing to put his city and his people above everything. Everything, Haemon. Everything. Though it costs you so much, this girl will be the last casualty of this war and the most important—for her crime reveals the moment in which we both grow up, together, Haemon, father and son. It hurts me as it hurts you. And that's the point. Suffering is the first rule of life for a man, because it burns out of us the instinct to cherish ourselves above the common good. It is a cure from within. And a man who puts himself, or anything before the welfare of his city, I say that man is nothing. I thank Antigone. She has awoken us in our apathy.

> HAEMON, *still and listening, attacks his father with great force—a brief and brutal struggle between them, bringing the* CHORUS

back into the square—until HAEMON *is pinned by his father on the concrete, restrained in a brutal military hold.* CREON *releases* HAEMON *as the boy stops struggling, trying to help him up, trying to repair the situation before a chorus of eyes.*

HAEMON: You know what I think? I think the way through this won't be directed by ministers and presidents, or kings, or priests. You're not in charge, you're *papier-mâché*, you can't stand up—it's up to us, we have to grow up ourselves, with our orphans' eyes, we have to see the way—

CREON: Oedipus only *saw* / once he'd suffered

HAEMON: Oedipus? What does that prove? He solved puzzles, he's good in a crossword crisis, but he wasn't a king, he led us *here*!

He wildly references the destroyed city that is his home.

And now you're king—

CREON: As *president* of a free government I will lead us, son / I—

HAEMON: No, you're a *king* … you'll be a good king … of an empty country.
You won't take her, Dad. I won't let you.

HAEMON *goes.*

CHORISTER: The man is gone, sir. And the boy is gone with him.
His pain is terrible.

CREON: Let him go.

Silence.

CHORUS: There are those in Thebes who …

CREON: What? Those in Thebes who what?

CHORUS: There is division, sir. About the girl. The public opinion is turning—

CREON: Opinion! Don't tell me what the *people are saying* as if that makes it a great truth. *Opinion* is the false shadow of a beast. We fear it only if we listen.

CHORUS: But a government must listen—

CREON: What, to the chirp, chirp about this little bird, because they feel sorry for her. And why? Because she's an attractive thing, isn't she? Bewitched *my* boy.
'Public opinion can force the lion through the hoop without the tamer cracking a whip.' [*Trying to recall*] Who said that?

Silence.

Not this lion. Not by that bird.
Where is she?
CHORUS: Under guard, sir, in your home.
CREON: Get her out! I won't have him see her. Get her out. Take her to the south gate prison.
CHORUS: It's in ruins, sir. It'll need demolition.
CREON: Not all of it.
CHORUS: Symbolically, it may not be wise.
CREON: Symbolically now?
CHORUS: We fought bravely in that area, sir. Women fought—civilian women. When the south gate broke, mothers and widows—teenage girls—took up our dead soldiers' weapons and from within that prison held back the insurgents. Eleven women died there. To incarcerate the girl in that prison would light a torch. Sir.
CREON: Brave women. Now take her to the cells beneath the ground, they're undamaged and empty.
CHORUS: They haven't been used for a hundred years, sir, they're like caves—
CREON: What, again, barbaric? You think me barbaric? You accepted this decree this morning, you all did. Now you blush at its execution.
CHORUS: We blush at its convention, sir. Under our new democracy—
CREON: [*correcting them*] Tomorrow!—

A stunned silence.

CHORUS: Tomorrow—yes …
We will be in violation of the Human Rights Convention.
CREON: We have the death penalty, it's a sovereign right, we won't abolish it in democracy. We're a shattered state—at the mercy of rebellion and civil chaos—we won't lose so strong a deterrent as the death pen—
CHORUS: Article Five of the Convention states that 'No-one be subject to torture or cruel, inhuman or degrading punishment'.

Brief silence. CREON *sits, starts picking at the food.*

How will she die, sir?
CREON: [*quietly, simply*] She'll go beneath the earth in the south gate cells. Tonight, she will receive a meal. And there will be no further contact with her. From anyone. Ever. [*To the* SOLDIER] Seal the door.

ACT ONE

CHORUS: Sir, surely our Constitution will not allow such detention—

The fury of the mind in CREON *now.*

CREON: *Our Constitution!* Sorry, do we have one? I didn't see one in my desk.

He finds a paper towel on his knee from the food.

Is this a Bill of Rights …? Oh no, it's a napkin! It is my vision will bring us one—from military dictatorship to democracy in a trice and through whose commitment? Mine. You think civil order will come from polite resolutions, written overnight? We are drowning, barely resuscitated. She knew the penalty, yet she decided to kick the world to pieces. She will be incarcerated. She worships the dead above the living … Well, once down there, death is a good option … I'll leave it to her discretion.

CHORUS: We would have you record our opposition to this decision—

CREON: Duly noted, here on the Constitution. [*Holding up the napkin*] Put her in the cells. Nothing gets in or out, she will choke on her own pollution, it will not infect our city or its *opinion*.

[*Handing back the food*] It's cold—

> CREON *exits. The* CHORUS *hold the gaze of the audience, inquiring of us, seeking our voice in response to the collapsing situation, while house lights rise to include us in the silent conversation— then darkness.*

END OF ACT ONE

ACT TWO

ANTIGONE'S LAMENT

We find ANTIGONE *in the palace, under guard of the* SENTRY. *The* SENTRY *is looking at family photos. A quiet calm.*

ANTIGONE: What happens now?
SENTRY: Wait.
ANTIGONE: Do we have to wait in here? We never come in here.
SENTRY: It's the only room in this palace with one door, this place is ridiculous.
ANTIGONE: I'm not going to run away.
    Beat.
SENTRY: I've seen 'em all. No-one wants to die.
ANTIGONE: I hate this room.
SENTRY: Should see my place!
ANTIGONE: What's gonna happen to me?
SENTRY: I don't know. I heard—under … I don't know.
    Why do you hate this room? This is a good room.
ANTIGONE: My father's reception room.
    This is the last place he saw.
SENTRY: Oh.
    [*Realising what that means*] Oh!
    It won't be long.
    Silence.
SENTRY: [*indicating a photo*] Is that him, your dad, when he was young?
ANTIGONE: My dad—my brother—depends how you look at it.
SENTRY: Oh yeah, that's awkward, isn't it? Sorry.
ANTIGONE: He was my brother, I suppose, when that was taken. My dad, once he married her. [*Pointing at another photo*] And they … made me. The bed's just in there if you want a selfie at ground zero. The most famous sheets in Greece—
SENTRY: She was beautiful. Jocasta. I saw her once, up close. No wonder she turned his head!

ACT TWO

ANTIGONE: Might have been easier for everyone if she hadn't.
SENTRY: [*another photo*] How old are you here?
ANTIGONE: Ten, eleven maybe.
SENTRY: I helped my dad build a house when I was ten. We had no money, but Mum made him build it anyway, any way he could. Nothing fit, the windows, the plumbing, the stairs. And I was his gofer. I hated it. Some days he'd go to town and give me chores to last a week, but I would just ... swim ... disappear in the sandpits, build fortresses and fight battles, I even cut a dress in half and strung it here, like a loincloth, nothing else—no-one saw me or anything. I'd seen pictures of the Iroquois, at the library, have you seen them? They could run barefoot on anything, never move a branch or snap a twig. And down in the mud clearings, down among the old rotting trees, was our favourite thing, *my* sister and I. Dragonflies. They're born in the mud, you know—they are the clumsiest bug—they struggle toward a tree that will take them to the sky for the first time, crawl then rest, crawl then rest, in dry little shells. We'd be so quiet, so quiet our ears hurt, if you disturbed them they wouldn't move. And when the moment finally came ... the tiny necks split open and they fall out, red and blue, so blue, sky blue, more blue than that, and just impossibly big from those little shells. And not clumsy anymore! But such a risky ride to get there. It's a miracle they grow up at all, a strong breeze can end it, they'll fall and get swamped by predators. When that happened we couldn't watch. It was like the opposite of a miracle. Whatever that is—

    HAEMON *enters.*

HAEMON: You can go, thank you.
SENTRY: No can do, sorry. Under orders. Been losing focus lately, gonna get it right from now on.
HAEMON: Then wait in the kitchen.

    She stays.

We can't get out of this room.
SENTRY: Well, what are you going to do? I'm not supposed to leave her.
HAEMON: Well, [*starting to undress*] I'm going to kiss her all over her body and we're going to make love, and you'll have to join us if you're gonna stay. Can't just stand on the *watch* all your life. Gotta muck in sometime.

ANTIGONE *laughs. Very quickly,* HAEMON *is naked.*

SENTRY: I'll be in the kitchen.

She goes. ANTIGONE *laughs harder.*

ANTIGONE: Don't come too near me.

HAEMON: Why not?

ANTIGONE: I'm dangerous to be near—don't touch me.

HAEMON: You never let me touch.

ANTIGONE: I know. My sister says I should. Let you. She thinks I'm scared.

HAEMON: You're not scared of anything.

ANTIGONE: Yes I am.

HAEMON: [*going to get a blanket*] I read a card on the wall near the old post box at the school this morning. It's become a bit of a shrine. Lost letters and photos of people missing. Must be a thousand letters, and ribbons, ten thousand, I don't know. There's one there from a kid in Melbourne, in Australia, beautiful little card, it came months ago, someone had opened it, put it on the wall, just a sympathy thing—he saw all the death on the news, the war. But he doesn't sign it. No name. He just says, 'I'm sorry, I can't put my name down in case they come and get me'. He's in Australia. Everyone's afraid, Antigone, not just you. The whole world's afraid.

Silence. She kisses him.

ANTIGONE: When we were kids, I always thought you liked her more. Ismene. Like everyone else. It was like growing up with—the sun … I don't know. She's beautiful.

HAEMON: Yeah, she is.

ANTIGONE: Go fuck yourself.

He kisses her, they move closer.

Will you help me? I don't really know what to do.

HAEMON: Neither do I.

She folds with him to the floor beneath the blanket as if to begin to make love and we are consumed by a choral ode. As HAEMON *continues in the shadows,* ANTIGONE *stands and moves among the* CHORUS, *as they enter. The moment is dark and suspended.*

ACT TWO

CHORUS: [*the women only*] Aphrodite immortal works her will on us all.
Even those who worship death will worship love.
A human life lasts but a day,
And still love spares not man or woman.
ANTIGONE: You're not really here, are you?
CHORUS: No. Your mind is always racing, girl.
ANTIGONE: You're talking to them, aren't you? I know they're there. I thought I could see them when Ismene was in the bath but I was just playing. But you can see them, can't you? The many eyes. *Now* they're looking at me, aren't they? Well, I'm gonna talk to them. Can I have some privacy?

She wraps a blanket around herself and then, very intimately with the audience, binds hers and HAEMON's *clothes into a makeshift noose. The* CHORUS *subtly move away. She speaks to us while making the noose.*

Who are you?
Are you the future—are they talking to the future, trying to teach you something? Or is it like history? Are you just recording it, all the sordid details—the inbred girl who ruined everyone's day—just recording it, for a library somewhere.
I know you're there.
And while my boy there, my love, makes a woman out of me, I'm gonna say a few things.

She watches him/them.

I wish I could enjoy it more but I have a lot on my mind—

She sits down.

So—this is my lament. My name is Antigone. [*A great vulnerability in her*] I wish I could surprise you and not die. But I know my destiny. Even my name means, 'worthy of one's parents' …! It's in my blood. I nearly gave blood yesterday. [*Showing us the black letters on her arm*] I chickened out, I thought if they tested my blood, they'd find I was prehistoric.
That's why I lied to Ismene when she asked where our father was. I saw my destiny, as we walked. He was spared the sight, lucky prick. Plague and death everywhere, bloated death. I told Ismene he died

happy, that he'd found joy; he didn't, he just screamed and screamed, like a child, the pain in his eyes. In the end I couldn't stand it, I just stopped walking, let go of his hand, and kept moving as he grabbed for me—like two kids playing blind man's bluff in the desert. He screamed some more—screamed my name—'worthy of one's parents', *'Worthy of one's parents!'*, that's all *I* heard—he cried for me and cursed me, but I just sat down and stared at a rock, just watched the sun move. People think I was loyal. But he was just a selfish old man.

[*Quickly now*] Not that my story is special. So many children have died here—there's nothing special about me. I hope the others get to talk to you too—but I just want to say this ...

There are three things I'll miss out on that I wish I could have. I'll never be married. I'll never make a child, my own little thing, to hold.

Looking back at HAEMON *who is moving under the blanket:*

Maybe there's a seed now, maybe my body is starting a process as we speak—as *I* speak.

Shielding her eyes from the light to look for the audience:

I hope someone's out there. Maybe it's happening already while he's inside me. Like how stars form—I loved this at school—molecular clouds—that's all pushing and pulling too. Gravity pulls in harder than the pressure is able to push out and the cloud collapses. Everything heats up and just gives way, there's no explosion, no great climax, that's a bit of a myth I think, things just ... happen at a steady pace ... and as it all dies down the hot core at the heart of the cloud sticks together, a little protostar—a thing that will *one day* be a star. Nothing much to look at, but one day ... like the dragonflies. The rest of the cloud doesn't go to waste either, all that dust makes comets and whole planets, whole worlds just from the *debris*, everything counts up there, every little thing—a promise, a dead brother—nothing goes to waste up there. Down here though ...

That's why I buried my brother, because, beyond the possibilities of my intuition, I knew what I did was right.

HAEMON, *gently, rhythmically moving beneath the blanket, groans as if almost reaching climax.*

Oh, he's finishing. I have to go. I want to say goodbye.

The third thing I'll miss? I just wanted to see what life was like—I kept waiting for a time when I'd see it, for myself—just to live. Goodbye.

She slips within him again and holds him as he comes.

Goodbye.

He doesn't answer. Their lovemaking, as it finishes, becomes like a dance, until the clothing is bound around her neck, and he holds her aloft, finding her dead body hanging above him, suspended in his own arms—a transformative moment.

Haemon? Goodbye.

HAEMON *screams, pulling her to the floor, trying to revive her. She is dead.*

FOURTH EPISODE

We find the town meeting set up, the stage covered in chairs, set up in circles, a beautifully organised, fluid image. An old blind woman, TIRESIAS, *is seated on one of the chairs, while a young* BOY, *around ten years old, is playing a game. He wears a set of wings from a dress-up shop and carries a weapon—the startling contradictory image of the child soldier. He is playing a game, walking across the bridges of chairs, moving behind the wall and reappearing on the other side. He stops to draw on the wall or screen, using his finger, big flourishes and small detailed strokes.* TIRESIAS *signs her dialogue to the* BOY, *who is deaf.*

TIRESIAS: That's it? Is that it? Good, step away, let me see it.
BOY: You can't see it.
TIRESIAS: Don't underestimate me, boy!
BOY: There's nothing there, we're just pretending.
TIRESIAS: Excuse me, you may be pretending, son, I'm not.
BOY: What are you doing?
TIRESIAS: Same thing you're doing! I'm imagining!
BOY: [*surprised*] What is it?
TIRESIAS: Well, I'm not gonna jump to conclusions, I'll just tell you what I see. I see wings, a tail, a long tail, I see a … couple of heads, or maybe they're big eyes, I think you rushed that bit, they're eyes, aren't they—it's very colourful—it's a bright blue wasp, a killer wasp, maybe a dragonfly, or a dragon?

BOY: It's a dog.
TIRESIAS: It is a dog indeed. Told you.

   The BOY *sits down.*

Well, don't rest on your laurels, paint over it, add to it—
BOY: I don't want to—
TIRESIAS: Start again—
BOY: No, I want to run. You said I would get to run!
TIRESIAS: Soon, darling. You will.
   You'll run.

      CREON *enters.*

CREON: Ah. Tiresias, I'm looking for my son.
TIRESIAS: You here for the town meeting? Poor showing so far, but this is progress, having you here. Haemon said you'd come. Would you like to take the floor first? No need to speak up, the boy's deaf.
CREON: There's no town meeting.

   He is leaving, no sign of Haemon.

You should visit the soup kitchen, you need a meal.
TIRESIAS: Oh no, I'm happy begging. Thebes is a beggar!
BOY: [*to* CREON *loudly*] What!?
CREON: [*gesturing somewhat feebly*] Oh. Ah. Kitchen? Meal—soup kitchen—
BOY: We do go to the kitchen. Every day. We sit together.
TIRESIAS: Sometimes.
BOY: Every day! [*To* CREON] We sit close together so she can pretend she's confused and take the food off my plate too.

   Silence.

I don't mind. She's blind. And hungry.
CREON: I'm helping there tomorrow, in the morning, I'll make sure you get double.

     CREON *again makes to leave.*

TIRESIAS: We shouldn't be, you know … a beggar. Thebes. Under Oedipus, when the plague came, and then in the early years of the war—
May I take the floor—?

She steps to the centre of the meeting hall, addressing a room full of empty chairs.

Honoured guests, Mr President, welcome—Tiresias; no fixed address, no fixed gender—Question for you, Mr President—We received thirty-six billion dollars in aid and development assistance over seven years—

CREON: Yes I know that, and I know what you'll say next too, you'll say, 'Where is it?'

TIRESIAS: Where is it? About thirty-six billion dollars of that thirty-six billion dollars is unaccounted for—

CREON: Yes, you're right—corrupt officials and generals, inefficiencies, no record keeping—that treachery is precisely what our new democracy will combat—

TIRESIAS: Ah, yes—tomorrow …

CREON: Yes. Tomorrow—Look—I'd like to speak with you, both of you—I have to find my son—could you come and see me tomorrow / at my office?

TIRESIAS: Oh, I'm not concerned about tomorrow. I can see everything tomorrow. It's today I'm worried about.

Anna Volska as Tiresias in Sport For Jove's 2016 production of ANTIGONE. *(Photo: Marnya Rothe)*

CREON: Come tomorrow—
TIRESIAS: Before you go, the boy has points of order too. He likes the art gallery, we went yesterday, didn't we, darling? He's a surprisingly good guide. The portrait room is untouched by the bombs, good news there, but the inventory of the sculpture gallery wasn't promising. What statues left, boy—?

The BOY *shrugs.*

Two headless nudes, life-size, and a man with no feet, but still standing! Pedestal gone, feet gone—still standing up! Amazing. The rest is carnage. It's a massacre in there. [*To the empty chairs*] Put arts funding on the list! Is someone taking this down?
CREON: Tiresias—
TIRESIAS: He's actually very good himself—show him, boy, show him your latest piece.

The BOY *unveils his invisible finger drawing on the wall.*

What do you think?

Silence. CREON *not in the mood for this.*

It's a dog.
BOY: No it's not, it's two eagles.

The BOY *runs off behind the wall, continuing his game.*

TIRESIAS: So it is! Sorry, I saw a draft.
CREON: You've spoken to him? Haemon. Did he say where he was going?
TIRESIAS: No. Shall I tell you what I see tomorrow?

The BOY *has reappeared from behind the wall in one clean movement, walking over the chairs. He is now ten years older, dressed identically.*

CREON: Where did the boy go? Where's that kid?
TIRESIAS: He's here. He's right there. Shall I tell you—?
CREON: No, it's a different …

He turns to the new BOY.

You, where did that boy go? The kid who went behind the wall? Is he your brother? What happened to him?
TIRESIAS: Here's what I see tomorrow—
CREON: When the boy comes back, you tell him to wait for me. I want to speak to him.

ACT TWO

TIRESIAS: He's deaf. You'll have to sign.
CREON: No, listen, be quiet, you can't see, it's a different boy, okay—
TIRESIAS: No, it's the same boy, Creon. It's you can't see—
CREON: No, there was a younger boy!—Forget it.
TIRESIAS: They grow up, you see.
They grow up so suddenly, you can miss it.

Silence. Confusion is beginning to shake CREON.

BOY: [*speaking loudly and signing*] I saw your son this morning. I told him I killed the old lady. I killed many enemies. He hugged me, he told me to wait here for the town meeting.
CREON: You're the boy?
Haemon … He said you were fourteen … when I came in you were, there was a boy—

The BOY *lashes out at* CREON, *strikes him violently to the ground.*

BOY: I'm not a boy. I'm a soldier!
CREON: What's happening?
TIRESIAS: This is the town meeting, your grace. We've been waiting a long time to be heard …

Silence—something is diminishing for CREON.

But we'll listen instead, if you want the floor …
You know what you need to say, I think. Now might be the time.

Silence.

Ye gods—I can't see, he can't hear and he won't speak—y'wanna throw us a bone—
CREON: [*shaken*] The floor is yours. What is it you want to say?
TIRESIAS: What is it you want to hear?
CREON: Don't play games with me, Tiresias—you think you know something I need to know, you tell me—say it—
TIRESIAS: [*tenderly*] You already know.
It's better if you say it …
CREON: That I'm wrong? What I've done today—you think I'm wrong?
TIRESIAS: No-one's thinking, no-one's judging— [*Calling to the room*] Anyone here judging? Hello?

Beat.

[*To the* BOY] We still alone?

BOY: Nobody here …
TIRESIAS: Hmm. You were right, kid, we needed posters—
CREON: You want me to say I'm wrong.
TIRESIAS: No, it's shady, it's murky … there's shade … thank God … we'd all overheat in that sun … but it's *you* ignored the shade. You stood with the boy, in the dust, you looked at him, before the dawn, in the shadows—and you were uncertain. So you waited for the sun to shine—the light makes things sharper, doesn't it?—hard edges, clear lines—and in that light, all of a sudden you were sure of yourself.

The older BOY *has run off again on his game.* CREON *has seen him go.*

CREON: What!? I should vacillate? Be indecisive?
TIRESIAS: No, but you could ask people … for counsel.
CREON: Don't give me fortune-telling, I'm running a *government*, I have counsel—
TIRESIAS: So do I.

The BOY *has returned seamlessly, now ten years younger again.*

[*To the* BOY] We fed our birds today, didn't we, darling?—in the park. Our little outlaws we call 'em, little villains.

CREON, *willing himself to leave, feels paralysed.*

CREON: Why am I listening to this—?
TIRESIAS: I held out the bread—they wouldn't eat! Bit my hands, tore the bag, wouldn't touch the food. I forced a bit of bread into one of them—chaos!—the others tore him to bits, screaming, wings snapping … sounded like books tearing, a whole library ravished …

She gently takes a piece of foil out of her mess of bags.

… the little one I fed, this little aristocrat, they assassinated him— Here he is— [*showing* CREON] part of him—we burnt him, the innards—the old ways, you know—
CREON: What are you doing—?
TIRESIAS: Showing you—just a bird. [*To the* BOY, *cupping the tiny body in her hands*] There's your next portrait, eh?—'Woman Holding a Small God'.
We tried to burn the innards—but no fire, no flame, nothing caught— just the smell of corruption, grey smoke, made us sick. You see, these

little exiles had already eaten. Gorged on the blood of the dead, a dead boy in a field, tried to carry him bit by bit to heaven I reckon— [*Whispering to* CREON] That's what I told the boy.

[*Sharply*] You left a dead boy above the earth and put a living girl beneath it.

CREON: I want my son—How long have I been here?—Where is my son?—

TIRESIAS: He's where you left him. Like this boy—like every child in this place—he's on the razor's edge—

Again the younger BOY *vanishes, replaced by the older.*

CREON: [*roaring at her*] Make sense! For god's sake, make sense! The edge of what?

TIRESIAS: Of fate.

He's out there right now, your son, in the dust—I can see that much—You can taste him, can't you? In your gut. You were so intent on winning an argument that you gulped him down, swallowed him whole. He's in the pit of your stomach, now he's going to dig himself in forever.

A good man yields when he knows he's wrong—can even give in to the dead.

CREON: What have I done?

Recognition has seized CREON—*a certainty of horror.*

The SENTRY *bursts into the room, crashing chairs aside. She is feverish and out of breath.*

SENTRY: She's gone. He took her. She was hanging— / She's gone, he took her down, he took her away—

CREON: Who? Haemon? Is she dead?

SENTRY: I don't know, he took her down—

CREON: Where is he?

SENTRY: I don't know.

CREON: *Where is he?!*

What have I done? [*To the* SENTRY] You, help me, we have to bury the body, then we find them— / We have to bury the boy first, Polynikes, get me a shovel, pick, anything, then we find my son, we'll find her, go—*Go!*

SENTRY: But Antigone, what if she's dead?

CREON *runs.*

TIRESIAS: Poor man. Hope he can run like you …
BOY: Can I follow him? Can I run?
TIRESIAS: Of course you can, son. Bear witness. Run.

The BOY *pursues* CREON, *fleet of foot.*

The CHORUS *moves among the chairs and clears the room, leaving us in a new space. We hear* CREON'*s voice screaming for Haemon at increasing distance, taken over by a woman's voice calling, 'Haemon!' —it is calm and practical.*

FOURTH STASIMON

CHORUS: War is the father of all things—Heraclitus said it.
O polemos einai pateras ton panton.
War is the father of all things.
Peace the mother.
She works to mend what he cuts to ribbons.
She fights shoulder to shoulder,
Soldier to soldier.
War is the father of all things.
Peace the mother.
A barbed-wired silence eats at their marriage.
This is our queen.
Dragging invisible bodies of the dead.
War is the father of all things.
Peace the mother.

FIFTH EPISODE

EURYDICE *has returned home at dusk from the hospital. She pulls a large trolley holding a mountain of surgical gowns, blood-soaked, a frightening image. She is calling into the house:*

EURYDICE: Haemon! Haemon! Where are you, darling?!
You said you'd help me with these!
Haemon!

Sitting among the mess, she calls again:

Creon!

A moment of peace. As she reaches into her gown pocket to find a cigarette, she pricks herself on a scalpel, absent-mindedly put there after rushed surgery, an exhausted oversight. She throws it the ground, she is not hurt. She lights a cigarette and looks at the fading light.

Days are getting shorter.

She flirts with putting the cigarette out on her arm as ISMENE *enters quickly, carrying towels to hang outside.* EURYDICE *is in immediate action as if never tired.*

ISMENE: Aunt!
EURYDICE: Oh, hello, sweetheart, help me get these into the laundry.

She hands ISMENE *gloves and a surgical mask. Their voices overlap sharply.*

ISMENE: Why do you have all this? / I don't want to touch these—
EURYDICE: Put these on, put these, put them on, Ismene.
I have to wash them by morning and get them back, we have nothing. / Thank god it's still hot enough to get them dry.
ISMENE: Why would they make you do it, / where are the cleaners—?
EURYDICE: The cleaners are dead—or missing. I don't know where the cleaners are, girl—annual leave?
ISMENE: Where are your security … / people?
EURYDICE: I sent them to give blood, I don't need them. / I'm doing the washing because we are privileged, Ismene.
ISMENE: You're a chief surgeon—
EURYDICE: The army kept my husband's electricity on, the hot water, everything, because we are privileged—the hospital's on generators, can't even run the coffee machine. That's why I have them—
ISMENE: Why do you need hot water? Can you wash them in cold water?
EURYDICE: Not these. They should be pathogen-treated, sterilised, but this is the best we can do. Who else has hot water? Come on—
ISMENE: I had a bath.
EURYDICE: What?
ISMENE: I didn't know. I had a bath, just now. I had a hot bath.
EURYDICE: You used the hot water? How long did you use the water? / Is the water gone, Ismene?
ISMENE: I don't know, / I think the hot water's gone—

EURYDICE: You think? You stupid, you stupid girl. You sit in a bath—you keep reheating a bath while half the city drinks sewerage and can't boil a kettle?
ISMENE: I'm sorry, aunty, I'm sorry I forgot. It's been a terrible day, aunty, / I wasn't thinking—
EURYDICE: Forgot! You've had a terrible day! [*Thrusting a bloodied gown in her face*] Are you clean now, you sterilised fuck, are you clean and perfumed—?

> *Beat.* EURYDICE *climbs down from her rage as quickly as she ascended, seeing the depth of* ISMENE*'s grief.*

I'm sorry, darling. Come on, stop—
ISMENE: I'm sorry—
EURYDICE: No, I'm sorry—Oh god—Wouldn't mind a bath myself. Come on, darling. I know. I'm sorry.

> *A peaceful moment, they sit together.*

I'm cranky—fighting a losing battle against surgeons I can't even see. Surgeons in the clouds—with their computer-guided bombs and precision instruments that come from—god knows where—It's so clean it's bestial. I wish they'd just sedate us all and get on with it.
I tried to stop it, you know, this war—convince my husband to accept terms, sue for peace, there's always a way if we can find it. I believe that. I even thought of the old ways—withholding sexual favours—but he never seems much interested anymore anyway.

> ISMENE, *sitting at her feet, reacts in embarrassment.*

Oh, grow up, Ismene, we're two girls talking. We can talk. There are too many secrets. You know what he said to me, two nights ago, before this final push? He said, we've lost this war. We've forgotten the *language*. We've stopped being aggressive and now we're getting hurt. And he felt it, I know he did. He told me once about Ajax at the battle of Troy, he was the toughest soldier in the Greek army, had to set an example, never show fear—his name was their battle cry—*Ajaax!* But he would weep! Behind his shield. Right at the battlefront, he'd weep behind his shield. No-one knew. Just him. And a piece of iron. Your uncle's the same. Refuses to show fear, won't use the word 'terrorist' because he can't admit to terror—but I've seen him. He's afraid. He weeps in front of me. Behind me, I guess. I'm his shield. Two nights ago he decided it was time to get aggressive again, to 'relearn the language', he said, whatever that means, killing I suppose. But when he gave the orders he cried all night in our bed. He knew he was going to hurt people I think, our people, and he wanted my approval ... not my opinion, just approval ... so he cried. I'm tired of being his piece of iron. You'd think at least a bedroom could be a democracy, a bedroom especially. [*Referencing the spattered surgical gear*] Half of this blood was spilt by our own bombs ... but shhh, I'm not allowed to say that, we have to keep a lid on that.

ISMENE: The radio said our bombs were ninety-eight per cent accurate.

EURYDICE: Ninety-eight per cent accurate! [*Laughing almost uncontrollably*] Well then, we're looking at the remains of some very unlucky people. What else the radio tell you?

I'm sorry, darling.

> *She kisses* ISMENE *and gets back to the task of carrying washing inside.*

I've had better days too.

ISMENE: [*almost to herself*] She's afraid too, I know she is. Why would he starve her, why does she have to die?

EURYDICE: Who?—What?

ISMENE: Antigone buried the body. She going to die, aunty. He's going to kill her—

EURYDICE: Whose body? Who's going to kill her? What?

[*Calling*] Haemon!

ISMENE: He's gone. He isn't here.

EURYDICE: Where's your sister?

ISMENE: I don't know. She was with the guard when I got in the bath, I heard Haemon come home, but then they were gone, I fell asleep I think—

EURYDICE: [*a missing piece setting in*] Gone where? What are you—?

ISMENE: Polynikes' body—can't be buried, Creon decreed it. But Antigone did it, she buried him in the dust, and said the words. He's going to starve her to death, you have to stop it, aunty—

EURYDICE: Where's Haemon? Where is he—?

ISMENE: You haven't heard any of this? / It's all today—

EURYDICE: No, I haven't heard any of this. / I've been in theatre, the phones don't work, I've been in theatre for thirty-six hours, girl— Where's Creon?
ISMENE: He's still at work—or he's looking for Haemon, / I don't know—
EURYDICE: Get me clothes— *Inside, get me clothes!*

> *As* ISMENE *runs offstage, the* BOY *is suddenly standing opposite* EURYDICE—*he comes from nowhere. It is the older* BOY *again. He is breathing heavily. As he is about to speak:*

Who are you?
BOY: I'm a runner. I ran so fast.
EURYDICE: Why, what do you want? I can't—do you need help?
BOY: Are you his mother? The unlucky boy?
EURYDICE: Who? Haemon?
BOY: The old blind woman said I'm a witness. That I must 'bear witness'. Tell only the truth, she says, always. Just find his mother and tell her what I saw, add nothing and leave nothing out, she said, like I do for her. She says I'm a lucky boy to see so well. Can I tell you what I saw? About the unlucky boy?
EURYDICE: Why is he unlucky—?
BOY: Because he's dead.

> *Beat.*

I followed the old man, he ran down the road and through the gates and out onto the plain. He didn't stop to pray where the soldiers are buried, where the flame burns all night. He kept running. When we reached the far side of the plain, we saw a big dog in the distance, it was getting dark but we could see it leaping and playing and chasing its tail. The man started shouting and throwing stones, trying to scare it away. So I ran faster, I was angry, I ran past him, I wanted to play with it. But as I got closer I saw it wasn't a dog—it was two eagles, and they were trying to lift an old tyre. I knew it was a tyre because we have them on our farm, it was black and curled and hard like the road. When we got close the eagles flew away, up into the sky, but they stayed there, right above us. I got dizzy looking up at them. When the old man tried to touch the tyre the birds came down again, they pulled it away from him, they didn't care he was there, screaming at them, they pulled the old tyre in two directions and it opened up, and I saw it had arms and a neck and a—it was a boy. His skin was black and rotting—his face was missing. I was so scared.

    TIRESIAS *has entered.*

The old man asked me to help but my chest was hurting. I said I would bear witness.

[*To* TIRESIAS, *quietly*] Was that wrong?

TIRESIAS: No, son. Go on.

BOY: The birds wanted the boy back, they whipped the poor old man with their wings, they tore his skin and clawed his mouth, he hit them and fought them until they sat in the air again, sat just above him, on an invisible branch, their wings were so big and slow, like blankets, I felt them in my chest. He cleaned the dead boy and sang to him, he hugged him—he cleaned the man then covered him with dirt—he was burying him.

Then I heard it. I heard it in my feet. Like a drum. The old man followed the sound through the dust to a hole in the earth, he was too tired to run, the birds had hurt him, so I walked with him, I helped him. We looked into the hole—the unlucky boy was there, deep in the ground, he seemed so far down, hitting the rocks with a pick, tearing the dirt. He was hitting so hard I could hear it in my feet.

The old man yelled a word: Haemon—he said, his lips were bleeding from the birds but I could still read them, he screamed—Haemon!—his teeth were red—but the drum kept beating. The man begged him to stop but when the boy looked up, when he saw his father, his eyes bright red, burning eyes, he screamed and threw the pick at the man, it fell down, he threw it again, he threw rocks and tried to climb and screamed at the man, 'I'll kill you! I'll kill you!' Then I saw the girl, there was a girl lying with him, behind him, in the giant hole, she was dead …

> *The* BOY *begins to grieve, unable to keep talking.* TIRESIAS *tells him to 'Bear witness'. As he begins to sign,* TIRESIAS *speaks for him, very matter of fact, just translating his statement, the* BOY*'s dancing hands the only movement on stage.* TIRESIAS, *seeing it without needing to look, knows the story.*

TIRESIAS: The unlucky boy stopped yelling—he kept digging—there was no sound anymore, no rock, it was soft now, his feet were gone, he

was still standing, but his feet were gone, the dirt was making bubbles around him. He kept digging, and he pulled at the walls where he was standing, and now his knees were gone, the man screamed for him to stop but the wall started breaking, the rocks. He was so calm. He lay down with the girl. He was looking up at us. Then my feet heard a big drum, and the hole swallowed them, like a big mouth closing, and they were gone.
The old man said to run—to run here. So I did.
BOY: Are you his mother?

Silence.

After a time, EURYDICE, *on the floor with grief, privately picks up the scalpel. As she walks into the home, the* CHORUS *begin to enter with a terrible keening/wailing, growing steadily to an extreme intensity, and she is plunged into darkness.*

EXODUS

TIRESIAS *and the* BOY, *the younger* BOY *again now, remain together in the empty space. They are waiting.* CREON *enters, in patches of moonlight, carrying* HAEMON, *dead, thick with dirt, the pair of them like clay statues. He is weeping. It is a catastrophe.* CREON *collapses, his son in his arms. There are bells at a great distance. We have travelled exactly twenty-four hours.*

TIRESIAS: Well, that's midnight. Long day!
[*Signing to the* BOY] The sun is a tortoise some days, isn't it? Long day.
There are the bells. [*For the* BOY *again*] The bells.
We now live in a democracy!
I feel better already.

She listens to CREON*'s quiet despair, his breathlessness, throat choked with the desert earth.*

[*To* CREON] You need a drink? Not much choice here …

She starts going through her bags.

There's a lot of wine, or a little water.

She pours CREON *water, holds it to him, he takes futile and desperate sips. The* BOY *starts searching her bags.*

You hungry, son? All that running.

She searches.

I have baby tomatoes. I pinched those, don't tell the man in charge. [*To* CREON] Our kids think tomatoes grow in supermarkets—d'you know that?—fifty-six per cent of them, it was in the paper. [*Signing to the* BOY] Hey, where do tomatoes come from?

BOY: [*eating a little tomato*] From the earth, they're the berries of a plant—they come from the nightshade plant. We had them on our farm.

TIRESIAS: Hmm. One of the forty-four per cent. Nice to make your acquaintance!

CREON desperately drinks from the cup again as she holds it to him, coughing, choking.

Not too much! The old Greeks had a word: *sophrosyne*.
Of the cardinal virtues, that was Apollo's favourite, back in the day. A 'saving mind', a mind to 'save' things, save them up, moderation, prudence.

CREON cradles the dead HAEMON in his lap.

[*Simply*] We are measured by the laws we break—by *sophrosyne*.
It's no-one's fault. We've always done it, Apollo knew that. Always excess. Look at this city. [*Taking in the landscape with* CREON] In ruins. And what do human beings do with ruins? We photograph them. Confronted with the wreck of whole civilisations we check our batteries are charged. We'll never learn. What goes up ... et cetera. [*Watching the* BOY *play*] Kids get it, they're baffled by tomatoes, but they have an instinct for gravity. The only thing they love more than building a sandcastle is jumping on it, taking it back to nothing. But then they grow up, they grow tall and they expect their pillars to stay standing too.
But now it's midnight. The dawn's coming—and the god of measure has awoken. *Sophrosyne* ...
And he brings music. Do you like music? Do you like Bach? He understood measure—balance. There's a cantata—*'Ich habe genug'*—I'll play it for you.

She takes out a small CD player from her bags and mess of materials.

I should have an oboe and a violin if truth be told, but beggars can't be orchestras—*'Ich habe genug'*—it translates roughly, no, literally, as 'I have enough'. What does that mean? 'I have enough.' I have it all? My time has been rich?

 CREON *openly weeps.*

No, I think you're right, it's darker than that, isn't it? The cantata. 'I *have had* enough'—that's it, isn't it? I have had enough. *Ich habe genug.* It's an ordeal and I'm tired of it …

He's not frivolous, Bach, he's preparing us to die.

We've been too casual with what we've been given, he says. We took everything—but we took nothing seriously—'Give me more,' we said, 'More for me, me', when the truth is—'I have enough'.

 She motions to the BOY *to press 'play' on the little machine. The lights slowly begin to fade as* TIRESIAS *exits.*

 The music is filling CREON.

 After a time, the BOY, *desperate to know what* CREON *hears:*

BOY: I can't hear it. [*To* CREON] Can you hear it?

 CREON *nods.*

How do I hear it?

 CREON *holds the* BOY, *great tenderness. He percussively demonstrates the sound gently on the* BOY*'s arm, then sways his body to the rhythm. The music swells to an immense scale, lights slowly taking the image to black.*

THE END